YOU ASKED FOR IT!

Strange but true answers to 99 wacky questions

Marg Meikle

Illustrated by
Tina Holdcroft

Scholastic Canada Ltd.
Toronto New York London Auckland Sydney
Mexico City New Delhi Hong Kong Buenos Aires

To Mac-a-doodle-doo, my bonny boy

Scholastic Canada Ltd.
604 King Street West, Toronto, Ontario M5V 1E1, Canada

Scholastic Inc.
557 Broadway, New York, NY 10012, USA

Scholastic Australia Pty Limited
PO Box 579, Gosford, NSW 2250, Australia

Scholastic New Zealand Limited
Private Bag 94407, Greenmount, Auckland, New Zealand

Scholastic Children's Books
Euston House, 24 Eversholt Street, London NW1 1DB, UK

Design by Andrea Casault

Canadian Cataloguing in Publication Data
Meikle, Margaret
You asked for it!

ISBN 0-439-98723-7

1. Questions and answers – Juvenile literature. I. Title.
AG195.M464 2000   j031.02   C00-930809-1
ISBN-13: 978-0-439-98723-3

9 8 7 6 5   Printed in Canada   06 07 08 09

Contents

Do dogs and cats have belly buttons?

and Other Amazing Answers About ANIMALS

Do dogs and cats have belly buttons?

Indeed they do. If you look — which can be tricky with all of that hair — it looks more like a scar, but it is a belly button. All mammals have a navel or belly button. It's the connection point for the umbilical cord that carries nutrients and oxygen from the mother to the developing baby. Once the mammal is born that cord isn't needed anymore because the baby gets its own oxygen and food. With humans, the cord is cut off and the short stump that remains dries up and falls off. The mother cat or dog chews off the umbilical cord and the stump will then also dry up and fall off. When a mammal is hatched from an egg, the way a platypus is, it also has a belly button/scar, but it is even harder to see. The scar is from where the developing animal was attached to the yolk sac inside the egg.

Why "innies" or "outies"? When the stump of the cord withers and falls off it usually leaves an "innie," or concave scar. But sometimes, because of how a baby develops and how the cord heals, it turns into a convex "outie" — which is no big deal. If it makes you crazy to have an "outie" you can get a plastic surgeon to change it when you are fully grown. But it's far easier just to count yourself special, since "outies" are far more rare than "innies." Take a poll with your friends and find out the ratio.

2.

Why are flies attracted to manure?

Ranteen B., Toronto, Ontario

Because manure is a favourite place for flies to breed. Flies like any decaying organic matter, such as decomposing grass, but manure has it all. It's nice and moist and warm — it's even edible! Manure is, basically, fly heaven.

Manure is a problem in horse barns, because stable flies also suck a horse's blood. This painful and annoying experience can drive horses into a frenzy, or even a stampede. Any horse subjected to this constant agony — even if it's only the hint of flies flitting around — can hurt itself by stamping its feet over and over again, damaging its hooves and joints, losing weight and getting sick.

Talk to anyone who works with horses and they will tell you that keeping the flies away is an ongoing battle. When you know that a 500-kilogram horse produces over 20 kilos of waste a day — that's over 7000 kilos a year — you can understand the importance of fly management.

The life cycle of a stable fly is around three weeks, from egg to adult. In her three-week life a female fly can lay 20 batches of eggs, with 40 to 80 eggs in each batch. Do the math. Each fly could lay 800 to 1600 eggs in less than one month. Think how many flies there are. If just half are females, each laying 800 to 1600 eggs during its life . . . It can quickly add up to millions, which explains why fly prevention rules.

So, what do horse people do? Get rid of the fly's breeding grounds and protect the horses from any flies that are around. For starters, keep the manure out of the stalls by cleaning it up daily. Usually the stalls get a big cleaning every morning and piles of droppings are picked up every two or three hours

3

— something horse people call skepping. You have to shovel droppings out in the pasture too. Then what do you do with it? Let it dry by spreading it out, or compost it so the flies won't want to hang around. Gardeners will love it!

Or, you could fight flies with fashion. There are fly masks made of mesh that let horses see and hear, but don't let the flies bite their faces. Mesh or fleece blankets or sheets and leg wraps are good, too, even a fringe that attaches to the bridle and swings as the horse moves, shooing away the flies.

Just in case you need to know: Horse people tend to call the fresh stuff "droppings," which becomes "manure" when it gets stomped into straw and shavings in the stall, or put into piles behind the barn.

3.

How did duck-billed platypuses get to look the way they do?

Natalie B., Innisfil, Ontario

Certainly in no obvious manner that anyone can figure out. At first glance, the platypus doesn't look or act like any other animal. The platypus is a monotreme — that's a mammal that lays eggs — which is rare to start with. There are only two other monotremes; both are species of anteaters found in Australia, Tasmania and New Guinea. Monotreme means "one-holed" because — unlike most mammals — the platypus uses the same body opening to reproduce and to eliminate body wastes. Aborigines call the platypus Mallangong, Tambreet or Boonaburra. Rock paintings of the platypus are estimated to be at least 8000 years old.

The scientific name for a platypus is *Ornithorhynchus anatinus*, which means "bird snout," for its rubbery duck-like bill. Its common name, platypus, means "flat-footed." Add the tail like a beaver's, the poisonous spurs, the fur coat, and the fact that it spends most of its time in water, and you see just how unusual platypuses are.

They are great swimmers, and although they're awkward on land, they live in underground burrows that can be up to 20 metres long. They can "roll up" the webbing between their toes to expose their claws for digging in a mole-like fashion. All of these features are combined in a package that is usually around half a metre long and weighs just over 2 kilograms — smaller than a domestic cat. So go figure on this beast.

Nevertheless, scientists have been trying to "go figure" for years. The first sighting of a platypus by Europeans was in 1797, near what is now Sydney, Australia. They thought it was a combination of reptile, bird, fish and mammal, so they sent specimens to England to be studied. People there thought it was a hoax, and one zoologist even tried to separate the platypus bill from its pelt. This specimen is in the British Museum of Natural History in London — you can still see the marks from the zoologist's scissors.

The platypus went against everything people knew about mammals. Mammals, as vertebrates, have backbones, so there it fits. But the platypus lays eggs. It feeds its young milk like other mammals do, but it has no teats. Instead it has slits in its skin where the milk seeps out. The babies suck on the mother's fur to get their milk.

So where did the platypus come from? There is not a lot to go on, as there have been only a few platypus fossils found. In 1971 two newly discovered platypus tooth fossils were estimated to be 25 million years old. After that, other fossils were found — a piece of jawbone, a hipbone and a skull. Then in 1984 a platypus jaw with three teeth was found in New South Wales. It is at least 110 million years old. This specimen is from the ancestor of today's platypus, and was named *Steropodon galmani.* In 1985 an almost complete skull of a fossil platypus was found. Then in 1991, two fossil teeth found in southern Argentina were estimated at 61 to 63 million years old. This is the only evidence we have that platypus-like creatures may have existed outside of Australia. (Scientists believe that at one time Australia was connected to Antarctica, and that was connected to South America.) Some scientists believe that the platypus is "the end of the line" for some of the very earliest mammals — mammals that had many of the characteristics we associate with reptiles.

The platypus is often thought to be primitive, but it's actually pretty "high tech." Its rubbery bill is covered with hundreds of thousands of sensors that are sensitive to touch and to the electric currents that are created by the movement of small prey like shrimp, insects, worms, shellfish, frogs and fish eggs. The bill is so sensitive that a platypus can even detect prey that is buried under mud or rocks.

However it got to look the way it does, this fascinating animal is worth a closer look. To do that, see the gorgeous photos and a robot platypus at the "Children of the Moon Platypus Burrow" Web site (page 155).

4.

Why is it called an earwig?

Get ready, because this is pretty gross. Way back in the seventeenth and eighteenth centuries, anyone who was fashionable in France and England wore wigs. Some of those wigs were big — up to a metre high — and they could get awfully warm after a day of being worn. At night the owners would put these enormous sweaty wigs onto a stand, and moisture-loving bugs would climb in for a good time. When the fashion victims put on their wigs the next day, the bugs would fall out. It looked like the bugs were coming out of people's ears, and that's how they got their name: earwig.

Okay, admittedly that's not the only explanation. Earwig is possibly just a poor pronunciation of earwing, which refers to the little ear-shaped hind wings of the insect, the ones that look like pincers. This probably explains why some people think earwigs can crawl into your ear, burrow into your brain and kill you. But that theory just isn't true.

5.

What colour is the axolotl?

Bethany B., Richmond, P.E.I.

If you think I'm making this up, think again. This is a legitimate question, but first let's tackle this question: what the heck *is* an axolotl?

It's a salamander that never changes into an adult, sort of like a tadpole that never becomes a frog. And it's big. Axolotls have blunt snouts and large mouths. They are not to be confused with mud puppies, although both creatures live in water and have feathery external gills. You can tell the difference because mud puppies have four fingers and four toes, but axolotls have four fingers and five toes. An adult can grow to 30 centimetres from its toes to the tip of its tail.

Axolotls stay at the larval stage for their whole lives, and they can even reproduce without having reached the adult stage. Scientists have found that they can make the axolotl metamorphose — change — into an adult salamander by injecting it with a hormone called thyroxin.

Axolotls come from Mexico, mostly in Lake Xochimilco, the lake that Mexico City was built on. The name comes from the Aztec god of games, Xolotl. It was believed he could transform himself into an axolotl to get away from his enemies. The ancient Aztecs used to honour axolotls, and eat them too.

What's their colour? Axolotls are darkish grey, mottled with green or occasionally with silverish patches. Their eyes are yellow with iridescent irises. Some axolotls, especially those raised in labs, have mutant genes that make them albino. These axolotls are all white, with red eyes. They are even creepier looking than regular axolotls.

6.

Why are people allergic to animal fur, but not human hair (considering humans are animals too)?

Kendra N., by e-mail

Allergies result from the way your body responds to the presence of foreign proteins, so the reason people aren't allergic to human hair is because it's not foreign. In fact, it turns out that people aren't actually allergic to any animal's fur, or even its feathers, but to the proteins that are present in its skin secretions, saliva and urine. Animals shed small flakes of skin called dander, and microscopic particles of protein are in the dander. The particles are so small they float in the air, and can stick to furniture, walls, clothes, carpets and so on. It's very hard to get rid of them. Then there are those other substances that people may be allergic to — pollen, dust and mould — which can cling to an animal's fur, especially if the animal spends time outdoors.

Some people think that dogs that shed less are safe for people with allergies. But allergists say there's no such thing as a non-allergenic cat or dog, since all dogs and cats have skin, saliva and urine. However, some breeds of cats and dogs may secrete less protein than other breeds, or a protein that a person is less sensitive to. The best pets for an allergic person are those that don't have hair or fur — like fish, lizards, turtles, salamanders and ants.

One-third of U.S. and slightly more than half of Canadian households have one or more cats. More people are allergic to cats than to dogs — around one third of all patients with allergies in North America are allergic to cats — and cat allergies tend to be more severe too. Cats have a special protein called "Fel d 1" that is often responsible for these allergies. This protein is transferred to the hair as the cat licks itself — something they do for so much of their day you could think of a cat as a "walking spitball." Since the hair they shed is covered in dried saliva, people with allergies can get reactions even when they don't handle the cat.

Female cats produce less than two-thirds of the Fel d 1 of male cats, and neutering a male cat decreases the level of Fel d 1 it produces. Unfortunately, for allergy sufferers, Fel d 1 can last for a long time — months or even years after the cat is gone from a home.

Dr. Stanley Coren, a professor of psychology at the University of British Columbia, did a study of people with allergies to their cats or dogs. Doctors had advised all 341 of the people he studied to remove the pets from their living areas. But only one in five of the study subjects followed doctor's orders.

What's the *strangest* thing people are allergic to? Would you believe water? There are only about 20 of these cases in the medical literature. The most recent is that of a Vietnamese man living in California. Since age 10, whenever he lets any kind of water (tap or sea water) touch his skin, he develops severe itching and white welts on his skin within five minutes, rapidly leading to a headache and severe respiratory distress.

Water is an essential part of the body, so it's almost impossible to avoid water touching your skin during the day. In fact, many people like sports involving water, such as swimming or surfing. But the young man in California quickly learned how to wash and dry himself very rapidly indeed. In his case, scientists have absolutely no idea what's going on. The man has no change in his blood histamine levels — a strong marker of an allergic reaction — and when scientists try treating him with various antihistamines, the drugs make absolutely no difference at all.

7.

Can animals be allergic to people?

There haven't been any significant studies done on this topic, but there is anecdotal evidence that animals might have allergies to people. A veterinary diagnostic laboratory in the U.S. tests dog and cat blood for antibodies to a variety of antigens. (An antigen is something that is foreign to your body.) One of the antigens they test for is human dander. Dr. Hugh Chisholm of the Atlantic Cat Hospital in Halifax, Nova Scotia, has a patient who tested "high positive" for antibodies to human dander. He says, "high antibody levels are interpreted by some clinicians to represent an allergic state. It may be possible that this cat is allergic to his owners!"

8.

Can an animal catch an illness from a human?

Kimberly B., Montoursville, Pennsylvania

Animals often get the rap for giving diseases to humans, but according to Dr. Hugh Chisholm at the Atlantic Cat Hospital in Halifax, Nova Scotia, it can also work the other way. Zoonoses or zoonotic diseases are those that can be transmitted between people and animals. The most common things transmitted from human to animal are parasitic, fungal and bacterial diseases, but in theory it's also possible to transmit viral diseases such as rabies. Common parasites that your pet could catch from you are *Giardiasis* (cysts in food, water, feces or soil), tapeworm (a flat worm that can grow up to 6 metres long), roundworm and scabies. Scabies is an infection caused by tiny mites that burrow under the skin and cause severe itching, scabs and hair loss. In animals it's called mange.

Then there is *Salmonellosis*, an intestinal bacteria that can cause severe diarrhea and fever (in humans we call it food poisoning), and ringworm — which is not actually caused by a worm, but by a fungus. It can easily be passed from human to animal. All in all, your pet shouldn't feel too confident about its health around you.

9.

If snow is so cold, why do bears and other animals hibernate in it? Wouldn't they get hypothermia?

Stephanie H., Caledon, Ontario

Hibernation is a way of surviving. When there's not much food and it's really cold out, sleeping through the winter makes lots of sense. Part of an animal's method of coping is to slow down its heart rate and lower its body temperature. Chances are that if you saw a hibernating animal you would have trouble telling if it was dead or alive.

Dr. Larry Wang, a zoologist at the University of Alberta in Edmonton (where it gets seriously cold in the winter), is one of the top international researchers in mammalian hibernation. He says "mammals don't usually hibernate in the snow. They have burrows underground, nests in hollow trees, or dens in caves or rock piles." He adds that the temperature in the immediate area around a hibernating animal is usually warmer than the surface air temperature, and that the surface snow acts as an insulator. "When the air temperature is −20° to −30°C in Alberta, the underground burrow temperature of the Richardson's ground squirrel is about 0°C." The animals need that snow insulation, because without it the burrow temperature could be even colder, causing the animal to either stop hibernating, or freeze to death while hibernating.

Hypothermia occurs when a warm-blooded animal's body temperature is "below the normal level or range [it] typically exhibit[s]," says Dr. Wang. So hibernating animals actually *are* hypothermic because their body temperatures are much lower than normal, around 0° to 5°C instead of their normal temperatures. (A steady body temperature is a feature all mammals share, but not all mammals have the same body temperature. Ferrets, for example, can range from 37.8° to 39°C, pigs are around 39.2°C, and cows can range from 37.8° to 40°C.) However, hibernating mammals can spontaneously re-warm themselves to normal body temperatures because they have internal heat-producing mechanisms, like shivering, that can operate even when their body temperatures are very low. We humans shiver when we are cold, too, but when we get to 32°C our bodies stop shivering and emergency treatment is needed.

Humans arc interested in animal hibernation because we can apply the information to medical treatments on humans. In brain and heart surgery, organs are now pre-cooled. Researchers have also figured out that the amount of blood reaching a hibernating ground squirrel's brain goes down by 90% or more from the amount circulating when they are awake and running around. Scientists are studying these animals to see how they handle reduced blood flow to the brain. What they learn may inspire ideas for new treatments for people who have suffered strokes, which usually involve an interruption of the flow of blood to the brain. Unlike human brains that have undergone a stroke, the brains of hibernating animals are not damaged by the reduced flow of blood.

Why don't birds' feet freeze in the winter?

Birds who don't take off to warmer climates in the winter have ways of dealing with the weather. Some grow more feathers, which they can fluff up for extra insulation when they need it. Like humans, some birds use shivering as a way to warm up — that movement increases heat energy enormously. And water birds paddle like mad to keep their feet from freezing into the ice. Almost all birds tend to stand on one leg a lot, holding the other up in their belly feathers to warm it. Where it is really cold, many birds go into a state of near hibernation overnight, which reduces their body temperature so they don't lose as much heat to the cold air.

The primary "bird trick" that makes the winter bearable is in the vein and artery system of the legs. The blood vessels going *out* to the legs run alongside the blood vessels coming *back*. This lets the cold blood of the limbs that are exposed to the cold "exchange temperature" with the warmer interior blood of the body, in a system that is more advanced than in humans. In this way there can be circulation of blood that is an even temperature, allowing the bird to keep moving — that's what keeps the brain and other vital organs going.

What would seem to be the most obvious example of really big cold feet is the Antarctic penguin. They use the heat-exchange system, as well as a clever way of varying the diameter of their blood vessels to control the rate of blood going to the feet.

Why do birds fly south for the winter?
Because it is too far to walk!

11.

Why are they called "Border" collies?

David G., Vancouver, B.C.

Have you ever watched a Border collie in action? Go, go, go. Work, work, work. Border collies need a job. That's because shepherds on the border of England and Scotland bred them to work herding sheep.

There have been sheep dogs for centuries, but the exact blend of characteristics that typify Border collies was finally arrived at in 1894, in attempts to breed dogs that were super-smart and very athletic. Now these dogs are herding livestock all over the world. Border collies love to take part in obedience and agility trials and Frisbee competitions, and they make great and loyal pets — as long as they are kept busy.

The name of a dog's breed often tells us a lot about it. For example, the German shepherd was bred in Germany in the 1880s to herd sheep — like the Border collie. But as the country became more industrialized there were fewer pastures to keep watch over. However, the breed's intelligence and other fine qualities convinced the police and military to use these dogs in their work. In fact, the motto of Captain Max von Stephanitz, the first breeder of the German shepherd, was "utility and intelligence." German shepherds have also been used as guide dogs for the blind since the 1920s.

During World War I, because of the negative association with anything German, the breed lost popularity. In the U.S. the name was changed to shepherd, and in England and Canada to Alsatian. But the soldiers returning from Europe were so full of admiration for the breed that even with the same anti-German sentiment during World War II, these strong and clever dogs were put to work as guards, mine detectors and messengers. The Americans formed an association called "Dogs for Defense," which provided thousands of German shepherds for service in the army.

Fido is a common dog's name. It means "faithful" in Latin.

12.

How come birds can stand on a telephone wire and not get electrocuted?

Heather J., by e-mail

To get a complete electric circuit, you need to touch two wires at the same time. If you look at the wires between utility poles, you see either two separate wires, or two together that are insulated. Either way, the bird isn't completing the circuit, so current can't flow. Some large birds, like condors or eagles, or even big fruit bats, can touch two wires with their two huge wings, and they *do* get electrocuted. It's estimated that in the U.S., about a million birds a year are killed this way.

13.

Why is a giraffe's tongue purple?

Tammy M., Cold Lake, Alberta

Purple or blue-black, the giraffe's tongue is enormous and muscular. It can be up to 54 centimetres long, and is designed especially to scoop up the acacia leaves giraffes love so much. That tongue needs to be strong, since the giraffe will often eat for 16 to 20 hours a day. A giraffe can maintain itself on less than 7 kilograms of leaves, but it often will eat up to 29 kilos of the feathery-looking foliage a day. But why is its tongue that colour?

It turns out that the tongue is probably purple for no good reason at all. Dr. Pat Carter, an evolutionary biologist at Washington State University, figures there was no evolutionary reason for the giraffe to have a purple tongue. The purple colour does not give the giraffe any better chance of surviving, so it really doesn't matter what colour it is. The tongue colour may be genetically linked to another trait that is uniquely giraffe-like, like its spots or neck length — the gene for a purple tongue might simply "come with" this other characteristic. This notion reminds us that not all traits have a "purpose." Dr. Carter says that there are some traits that seem to be random, and make no difference to how the animal survives — maybe the tongue colour of the giraffe is one of them.

However, Brian Keating at the Calgary Zoo thinks the dark tongue colour might be a form of sun protection. Because the giraffe's tongue is outside of the mouth so much (eating all those acacia leaves) this theory makes sense, though so far there is no way of knowing for sure.

Other animals with purple or blue tongues are the Shar-Pei dog, the Blue-tongued skink (found in Australia, Tasmania and New Guinea), and the Chow Chow dog. A fable about how the Chow Chow got its blue-black tongue goes like this: When God was painting the sky blue, He spilled a few drops of paint as He worked. The Chow followed after, licking up the paint — and from that day on the Chow Chow had a blue tongue!

Giraffe Facts:

- Giraffes are mostly quiet beasts, but when they do make mouth noises, they can moan, moo or snort, as well as grunt, bellow or bray.
- Every giraffe has a different set of markings.
- Giraffes have seven vertebrae in their huge necks, the same number as humans.
- The average male giraffe is 5.3 metres high — about three times the height of the average man.
- Giraffes aren't keen on lying down: they sleep and even give birth standing up.

**When do giraffes have eight legs?
When there are two of them.**

**Why didn't they invite the giraffe to
the party?
He was a pain in the neck.**

**Why are giraffes so slow to apologize?
It takes them a long time
to swallow their pride.**

If the dinosaurs died out because of the asteroid that hit Earth, why did the mammals survive?

Kaiwei G., Coquitlam, B.C.

Scientists have been debating how the dinosaurs became extinct for decades, and the debate will probably continue as paleontologists continue to make new and startling discoveries.

From the fossils that have been found, scientists believe that dinosaurs appeared at the beginning of the Mesozoic Era (245 – 208 million years ago), and were the most common form of animal life for the next 160 million years. Then about 65 million years ago, the dinosaurs disappeared. But why?

Russell Jacobson, a paleontologist/geologist at the Illinois State Geological Survey, maintains an information-packed Web site that provides some answers. According to Jacobson, there are two main theories about how the dinosaurs died out. Some scientists believe that it happened gradually over a long period of time, and that dinosaur populations were on the verge of extinction before any catastrophe happened. Other scientists believe that dinosaurs disappeared suddenly when the Earth collided with a comet or an asteroid about 65 million years ago. The explosion caused a period of darkness and acid rain from the soot and dust in the atmosphere, which in turn caused climate changes and affected the dinosaurs' food supply.

Scientists believe that there have been at least five mass extinctions, where about 60% of all known plant and animal species disappeared in a short time. But even though we call it extinction, dinosaurs didn't completely disappear. Some of them evolved into a group of animals that are now present in almost every environment — birds.

So, recognizing that some groups of dinosaurs did survive, it's easier to understand that other species could also adapt and survive. Some of these animals might have burrowed underground — maybe to enter a sort of hibernation period — and many of them were scavengers who could live off the carcasses of dinosaurs or other animals.

Other scientists believe that the major groups of mammals were around long before the dinosaurs disappeared. There were small marsupials (animals that raise their young in a pouch, like opossums) and insectivores that were similar to shrews and hedgehogs. But it was only after the dinosaurs disappeared that the mammals became the dominant land animals. Within 10 million years of the dinosaurs' disappearance, mammals of every kind were living on the land, in the seas and in the air.

• The word dinosaur, meaning "fearfully great lizard," was first used in 1842 by Sir Richard Owen.
• The person who discovers a new dinosaur usually gets to name it. The name might describe how paleontologists think it behaved (*Tyrannosaurus* means tyrant lizard), or the place where the fossil remains were found (*Albertosaurus* was found in Alberta), or how it looks. Some are named in honour of a person (*Stokesosaurus* was named for Lee Stokes, a famous American paleontologist). One of the most unusual names is *Irritator* — because the people who found the fossil made it look different by adding plaster to the bones. That really irritated the paleontologists.
• Dinosaurs ruled the Earth for about 160 million years. Modern humans have been around for less than 300 000 years.

Why is it that the female lion does the hunting and not the male lion?

Tammy M., Cold Lake, Alberta

It is purely a matter of body dynamics. The females are slimmer and they can move faster. They are truly great hunters, and without that huge mane, they can hide more easily. (Just imagine a male lion hiding behind a tree! His mane would give him away.) Besides, the male is busy guarding the hunting area for his family.

16. How do worms see in the dark underground?

They don't, because worms have no eyes. They simply move slowly and feel their way around. Despite their lack of eyes, they do sense the light, because they have light-sensitive organs on their heads and tails. Why do they care about light if they can't see? Sunlight would dry out their skin and eventually kill them, so that's why they live underground.

And what do worms eat down there? Way down deep they go for raw dirt and ground-up minerals. According to Mary Fauci, an agricultural researcher at Washington State University, worms living near the soil surface eat organic matter like fallen leaves and dead grass. They also eat the small organisms like bacteria or fungi that live on plants. She adds that as well as eating, they excrete (or "cast," as the gardening industry puts it when it is trying to sell worm castings). These castings are very nutritious for plants. That's why you want worms in your soil and in your compost.

Why and how do cats purr? And why do they hate water?

Rory V., Vancouver, B.C.

There are theories galore, but no one has really nailed it. Here are a few of the better ideas:

Why?

- Purring is a good way for mother cats to communicate with their young. Newborn kittens can't see, but they can feel the vibrations of mom purring.
- It's a sign of contentment. A mother's purring tells her kittens that things are fine, and a kitten nursing can purr to the mother to say the same thing.
- Sometimes cats purr to calm themselves down when they are stressed, like while they are giving birth, or while injured, dying or just frightened.
- Sometimes cats just want to purr — it isn't a reflex, it is a voluntary act.

How?

- By drawing the vocal cords (or bands) together and apart 25 times a second.
- By vibrating the membranes, called "false vocal cords," which are the fleshy folds that are behind the cat's real vocal cords.

Cats can vocalize more than a hundred sounds, but dogs can only come up with ten.

Now to the second part of the question: Why do cats hate water? Not all cats hate water, but most do. There's a breed called the Fishing Cat, that's found from northern India to southeast Asia. It's such a good swimmer that it will dive into the water and go after fish. It will even get low enough in the water to grab a duck from underneath! Then there's the Turkish Van, which loves to takes baths — and will jump into your tub or a lake to do so. This very large domestic cat seems to have a virtually waterproof cashmere-like fur, mostly white with rust or blue/black around the ears and on the tail.

Cougars will swim across small lakes and cross streams — they just look for a shallow spot. Some of the big cats that live in hot climates, like tigers, lions, jaguars, ocelots and jaguarundi, seem to love water.

But that's just two very rare breeds and some really big cats. Does the average domestic cat hate water? Catherine Ulibarri, a veterinary professor at Washington State University, has a theory that because fur is animals' protection against the cold, they try not to get it wet if it could cause a problem that would threaten their survival. So domestic cats and big cats that live in cold climates, like lynx and bobcats, will avoid water.

Not all domestic cats actually hate water. Dr. Janice Crook, a veterinarian in North Vancouver, was treating a big tabby cat named Johnny, who'd torn a ligament in his hind leg. When asked how it happened, his human said that Johnny had slipped while getting into the shower — he and Johnny shower together every morning!

Where do cats like to swim?
In the puss-ific.

What do you call a cat that swims
in the ocean?
An octo-puss.

When is it bad luck to be followed by a
black cat?
When you are a mouse!

18.

Why do dogs chase cats, and why do cats and dogs fight?

MatrixE, by e-mail

Dogs don't chase cats simply because they are cats. A squirrel would do nicely. We simply associate dogs and cats since they are both pets. We even have a phrase for it — "fighting like cats and dogs."

Dogs instinctively chase small animals. It's part of their programmed need to hunt, called "prey drive." Dogs are predators, and movement triggers their instinct to hunt even though we feed them good food and they don't actually need to hunt at all to survive. Certain breeds of dogs were developed for particular hunting qualities. Terriers were bred to kill rats, for example, and retrievers were bred to be assistants to their masters in hunting. They will gently pick up the prey and bring it back to their master.

You can train your dog not to chase cats, but without such training dogs will always go after them. Most trainers think it's a good idea to teach your dog that cats are off limits at all times. Teach your dog "No" or "Leave it," and say it whenever it chases a cat. A water gun also comes in handy — just squirt the dog when it chases after a cat, to distract it.

If dogs and cats are raised together they will usually get along well. They will play, sleep together — even share the same water bowl. But introducing a dog into a cat's household, or a cat into a dog's household, might lead to problems. And even if a dog gets along with its own feline housemate, it might chase other cats when it encounters them outdoors.

19.

Why is a hoot or hiss called a catcall?

You know the sound — a whoop, or a high-pitched hoot or whistle that is made by an audience that doesn't like what it's watching. At least, that's the way it is in Britain. In North America, catcalls have come to mean an audience likes what it's watching. Go figure.

Why is it called a catcall? It started in British music halls, inspired by the cry of a cat in distress. Back in the 1600s people used an actual whistle to show that they weren't keen on what they were watching, or that they were bored with the show. Eventually this gave way to people sticking their thumb and forefinger in their mouth and whistling to imitate the sound of the actual whistle.

A hiss or catcall can be pretty rude, but it's not as bad as pelting a performer with rotten vegetables. That used to be a way of expressing disapproval in the days when William Shakespeare was writing and performing plays.

20. How much wood would a woodchuck chuck if a woodchuck could chuck wood?

According to Cornell University, a woodchuck would chuck about 315 kilograms (if it could). They say that compared to beavers, groundhogs/woodchucks are not adept at moving timber, although some will chew wood. A wildlife biologist once measured the inside volume of a typical woodchuck burrow and estimated that — if wood filled the hole instead of dirt — the industrious animal would have chucked about 315 kilograms worth.

21.

What does "a murder of crows" mean, and who makes up these names?

These group terms are often called collective nouns or nouns of assemblage. James Lipton, in his excellent book, *An Exaltation of Larks*, prefers "terms of venery" — venery in this sense referring to hunting, because the originators of the phrases were word hunters, collectors of language subtleties and delights. Many of these collective nouns, like "a pride of lions," are centuries old, but more show up every day.

Who makes them up? Anyone. *You* could! Think about a group of things, and how they sound or look or act, where they live, or something special about them. You could be the originator of "a pocket of Pokemons" or "a slew of skateboarders."

Here are some favourite collective nouns:

a kindness of ravens
a rafter of turkeys
a skulk of foxes
a peep of chickens
a trip of goats
a paddling of ducks
a parliament of owls
an exaltation of larks
a congress of baboons
an army of caterpillars
a float of crocodiles
an ostentation of peacocks
a prickle of hedgehogs
a crash of rhinos

Why do people wear underwear?

and Other Crazy Facts About CUSTOMS

22.

Why do people wear underwear?

Sarah B., Cou, Kentucky

Basically, to cut down on laundry. It's just a layer between your skin and your clothes that helps keep your clothes clean. And it's not even a new idea. Loincloths are underwear, and they were popular in Crete 4000 years ago. It's hot there, so decorated loincloths were often the total outfit. There are also records of the Egyptians wearing material tied around the body, under their clothes, as far back as 3000 B.C. As time went on, women took to wearing short skirts as underwear, and around 200 A.D., the forerunner of the brassiere showed up, a sort of breast band, called a *strophium* or *mamillare*.

People didn't really call it underwear until 1879. In late 1849, Amelia Bloomer started *The Lily*, a newspaper designed to inform women about their rights. She supported the idea of wearing an outfit comprised of a skirt below the knee, with long, full, ankle-length pants or pantalettes underneath. Her aim was to free women from having to wear restrictive clothing. Eventually such pants were called "bloomers" despite the fact that the fashion was a failure at the time. Today some people call any baggy undies "bloomers." The garment that we now call women's underpants didn't really come along until the early 1900s.

Longjohns is a word that comes from the world of boxing. In 1889 John L. Sullivan, a boxer who always wore long underwear pants (or should we call them undershorts that were long?) became the last Bare-Knuckled Champion of the World. (Why bare-knuckled? His 75-round knockout of Jake Kilrain at Richburg, Mississippi, on July 8, 1889, was the last heavyweight title bout under the

London Prize Ring — or bare-knuckle — rules.)
Since John L. Sullivan was so famous, his
underwear became known as John L's or Long
John's, until they eventually lost the capitalization
and became just longjohns.

Undershirts and tank tops were a big step for
women's freedom from fashions like corsets — a
tight-fitting support undergarment that included
metal or whalebone "stays" (supports) that were
laced up tight to narrow women's waists and
"improve their figures." Such clothing wouldn't let
women move or breathe freely or play sports easily.
Less restrictive undergarments like undershirts
came along in the mid 1800s – but for sports only.
By 1900 there were fancier silk and lace versions
for women, and plain shirts for men. By the 1930s
the bra won out for women, and by the 1940s and
1950s it was mostly men who wore undershirts.

• Underpants are also called: skivvies,
unmentionables, panties, bloomers, undies,
knickers, drawers, gaunchies, step-ins, scanties,
unwhisperables, small clothes, inside
clothes and underpinnings.
• Did boxer shorts come from the world of
boxing, too? Could be. Some people think that
boxer shorts came out of the ring and onto
men's bodies as underwear early in
the nineteenth century.
• Nowadays there are boxer short styles for
women, a fashion that dates back to times when
women's undies were looser, not fitted
as they are today.

23.

Why do they call T-shirts T-shirts?

Zavh T., by e-mail

Here's the answer: because they are shaped like a T. Today in the U. S. the T-shirt industry sells over a billion dollars a year in printed T-shirts. They started out as underwear, but in the summer heat of World War I, American soldiers in Europe were allowed to wear lightweight undershirts as shirts. Compared to their hot wool uniforms, this seemed like a dream come true. By the time World War II came along, the T-shirt was the norm for the troops.

It took the movies to get the public involved. When John Wayne and Marlon Brando wore T-shirts in the movies in the early 1950s the public was shocked. But in the 1955 movie *Rebel Without a Cause*, when James Dean — the coolest guy ever — wore a T-shirt under an open shirt, the world took notice and the fashion took off. Hippies in the 1960s took to tie-dyeing T-shirts, and as silk-screen processing became more advanced, printed shirts took off too. Nowadays T-shirts are everywhere, and everyone has a drawerful.

Here's an idea for saving your favourite-ever T-shirt: turn it inside out, and sew up the arm holes and the bottom. Then turn it right side out again, stuff it with polyester fibre-fill and hand-stitch the neck closed. Now you've got a great pillow that carries your own memories, and is cozy to boot.

**What kind of shirts do golfers wear?
TEE shirts.**

24.

Why do people clink glasses before they drink?

This custom comes from the days when folks —
in particular, Greeks and Romans — didn't trust
each other too much. In fact, toasting today is a
custom that survives an ancient "mutual trust"
ceremony. Poisoning was fairly common in those
days. (Want to get ahead in the world? Knock off
your opponent.) So here's how people made sure
they would come out alive from a social event: pour
a little of your wine into your fellow drinker's
glass, and vice versa, to seal the deal. Since you'd
each have part of the other's wine, there's no way
you would poison him or he would poison you.
This became such a custom that even friends would
do it. And of course, when the wine exchanged
glasses, they would clink a bit.

Making glass clinking a custom came with the
early Christians. If you are giving someone good
wishes and you both have a glass in your hand,
you might as well *do* something with that glass.
Besides, the Christians thought the clinking of
the glasses sounded like church bells. Also, being
superstitious, they felt the sound could scare away
the devil. So the clink "boosted" the good wishes.
Along with your toast — "cheers," "Here's mud in
your eye," "*skål*," or whatever — you would clink
your glasses together. The Christians called this
"the kissing of glasses."

So what about the wacky tradition of clinking
glasses at a wedding reception to get the bride and
groom to kiss? It's like a toast (a term that comes
from when the Romans would flavour their drinks
with spiced toast) but it's a shortened version. And
it's not new. You can read about the whole clinking/
kissing thing in *The History of the Kings of Britain*,
written by Geoffrey of Monmouth in 1137.

Geoffrey writes about a banquet in 450 A.D. where it might have all started, but in a reverse sort of way. At that banquet King Vortigern kissed someone he was interested in marrying after he made a toast, and married her that evening. Now you have to wait for the reception to do the clinking/kissing.

Here's "Here's to you!" or "To your health" in other languages:

British: *Cheers!*
Chinese: *Wen Lie!*
French: *A votre santé!*
German: *Prost!*
Greek: *Yasas!*
Hebrew: *L'Chayim!*
Hungarian: *Ege'sze'ge're!*
Gaelic: *Sláinte!*
Italian: *Alla Salute!*
Japanese: *Kanpai!*
Polish: *Na Zdrowie!*
Russian: *Za vashe zdorovye!*
Spanish: *Salud!*
Swedish: *Skål!*

Why do people go all out for the sixteenth birthday of a child and not the fifteenth or fourteenth or any other age? Shouldn't you celebrate the 18th birthday, considering that that's when you become an adult?

Elisabeth M., Ontario

Throughout history, every culture has had its own way of marking the different stages in the life cycle. Sociologists and anthropologists call these rites of passage. The transition from childhood to adulthood is certainly a stage worthy of acknowledging and celebrating, but *when* to do it has varied greatly.

One example comes from the Jewish tradition. For Jewish boys, 13 is the most important birthday. A Bar Mitzvah is held on the Sabbath nearest the day a boy turns 13. At this age, the boy is considered to be responsible for himself and his actions before God and his fellow man. Jewish girls have a similar ceremony, a Bat Mitzvah, on their twelfth birthday.

In England up to a few generation ago, and in France, nobles presented their daughters to the reigning monarch when they were about 16, to show they were old enough to become socially active — that is, marriageable.

In 1748 in the U.S., a similar ritual of presenting young women "to society" began with 59 colonial Philadelphia families holding a "Dancing Assembly," which eventually became known as the "Debutante Ball." The "Deb" Ball was a chance for young women to be introduced into society — and to eligible young men from "good families." These balls were usually very elaborate, and extravagant gifts were showered on the young ladies.

The expression "Sweet Sixteen and never been kissed" was tossed around with lots of giggles and blushing. But it was a serious thing. By the 1920s some families gave an extra present if the young woman could answer affirmatively. In some parts of the U.S. — even in a few places in Canada, such as military bases — debutante balls are still an important part of a girl's life.

In Latin America girls look forward to their *fifteenth* birthdays. A girl's entrance into womanhood and her eligibility for marriage is celebrated at her Quinceañera (also known as the Quince, or Quince Años). In the beginning the Quinceañera symbolized a girl's time of renewed devotion to the church, but in more recent years it has been celebrated as the age at which she is old enough to begin dating. The event can be as elaborate as a wedding. Attendees wear gowns and rent formal wear, and there are limousines, photo sessions, catered dinners, dance parties and arranged flowers. This is a serious rite of passage to mark a special day that happens once in a girl's life.

As for when you become an adult, you can drive in most places at age 16. You can vote at age 18 in many countries, although it is still age 20 in Japan. In Russia, a person is issued an internal passport by the government at age 16, to recognize that they are now considered an adult. Still, it is more commonly believed that you have to be 21 to have reached maturity.

Why? Tradition. In Britain a person "comes of age" at 21, and this has been the case since the Norman invasion in 1066. It is thought that this was because the 13- and 14-year-olds who had been going into battle were far too young. They didn't have the strength to wear armour or to carry a huge lance. Age 19 was used next, but it was upped to 21 for reasons which seem really wacky today. In the days when a 19-year-old inherited property, it could take a couple of years to deal with the paperwork, so — according to one source — the age of maturity was just bumped to 21 to make all the legalities easier.

- In ancient times a birthday was considered to be the only time a person could be helped by good spirits or harmed by evil ones. Relatives and friends would bring the birthday boy or girl good wishes, thoughts and gifts to ward off the evil spirits.
- Birthday parties or *kinder feste* were invented in Germany. For that day the child was the centre of attention and got gifts from family and friends.
- Ancient Greeks celebrated the birthday of Artemis, Goddess of the Moon, and likely invented the birthday cake by their custom of bringing cakes to her temple. The cakes were round, in the shape of the full moon, and were decorated with candles representing the moon's glow. We probably got the idea of making a wish and blowing out the candles from the time when people thought that the smoke from a fire could carry their prayers up to the heavens.
- Driving away evil spirits was an ongoing theme. That's what birthday smacks, pinches, spanks or bumps are for. In Belgium this goes even further — the families of birthday children will sneak into their bedrooms in the morning and prick them with a needle. But the birthday kids better brave it out. Some believe that if they cry then, they will cry all year.

Does a cow's tail facing east mean rain?

and Other Weird Info About WEATHER

Does a cow's tail facing east mean rain?

Leanne S., Windsor, Ontario

This was a really long question. You also asked if it was true that crickets chirp faster in warmer weather . . . that a cow's tail facing west means clear weather . . . that turtles crossing the road means a dry spell is on the way . . . and that *broad* brown stripes on a caterpillar mean that the winter will be mild, but that *narrow* brown stripes mean it will be a terribly cold winter.

Any of these *might* be true. And then again, they might not be. Much of this can be considered superstition, and much has been debunked by scientists. But you can't knock the fact that for centuries and centuries farmers and shepherds and herdsmen — basically, people who hang out with animals and insects and birds — realized that these beasts often know when a change is coming. It also makes sense that animals would be equipped with sensors, since they need to know if a coming storm could rob them of their next meal or wipe out their nest. Generally, it has been observed that animals become unusually restless before dangerous weather, and that they tend to eat more too.

Naturalists are out there collecting all sorts of information on the behaviour of animals. How animals act when the weather changes is one of the things naturalists watch for. Here are some observations from a book called *Weather Lore: a Collection of Proverbs, Sayings and Rules Concerning the Weather* by Richard Inwards, first published in 1893:

- If animals crowd together, rain will follow.
- When a cat sneezes, it is a sign of rain.
- If horses stretch out their necks and sniff the air, rain will ensue.
- Hark! I hear the Asses bray;
  we shall have some rain today.
- It will rain if bats cry much or fly into the house.
- Turkeys perched on trees and refusing to descend indicate snow.
- Magpies flying three or four together and uttering harsh cries predict windy weather.
- Porpoises in the harbour indicate a coming storm.
- Air bubbles over the clam beds indicate rain.
- When the glow-worm glows, dry, hot weather follows.
- The louder the frog, the more the rain.
- Wasps building nests in exposed places indicate a dry season.
- Spiders work hard and spin their webs a little before a wind, as if desiring to anticipate it, for they cannot spin when the wind begins to blow.
- A fly on your nose, you slap, and it goes.
  If it comes back again, it will bring a good rain.

And one more thing. Cricket chirping is not a prediction of what the weather *will be*, but it is a reading of what the temperature *is*. The formula is this: Count the number of chirps in one minute; divide the number of chirps by 4, then add 40. That number will be the temperature (in degrees Fahrenheit),or pretty close to it. Check page 155 for a Web site that includes a Cricket Chirp Conversion Calculator.

27.

Can you really tell what spring will be like from whether or not a groundhog can see its shadow?

Well, that's how the story goes, but let's see if it is true. We call February 2 Groundhog Day, but it was originally called Candlemas, a Roman Catholic celebration day for the Virgin Mary. Even then, there was a weather connection:

> If Candlemas Day be fair and bright,
> winter will have another flight.
> But if it be dark with clouds and rain,
> winter is gone and will not come again.

Or,

> If Candlemas Day be bright and warm
> Ye may mend yer auld mittens
> and look for a storm.

In terms of astronomy, February 2 is called a "cross-quarter" day. It is halfway between the winter solstice in December and the vernal equinox in March. So perhaps Candlemas was like the balancing point of a see-saw — the weather could go either way. What isn't clear is why good weather on that day means bad weather to come, and vice versa.

And what about the groundhog connection? Well, in parts of Europe people also watched the local hibernating animal (hedgehog or bear or badger) to see when it emerged from its winter sleep. If the weather was clear and sunny on Candlemas, people would say that seeing its shadow had "scared" the animal back into its den. German immigrants brought this custom with them to North America and — since we are relatively hedgehog-free — they connected it to woodchucks (also known as groundhogs), which are well-known hibernators. These are the animals that you hear about on Groundhog Day.

Canada's official groundhog is Wiarton Willie. Willie's U.S. counterpart is Punxsutawney Phil. On Groundhog Day in the towns where Willie and Phil reside, there are huge parties, and the animals' "predictions" are broadcast across their respective countries.

But how accurate are they? A study in Canada over a number of decades in a number of cities gave the groundhog only a 37% correct score. And in the U.S., Phil's record isn't so hot either. Records from the National Climatic Data Center in Asheville, N.C., show that since 1887 Phil has only been right about 39% of the time. At the Oklahoma City Zoo the task of predicting the weather has gone to a pair of potbellied pigs, Bea and Kay. So far Bea and Kay are 0–4 in weather prediction. It's enough to make you think that you'd get a better prediction if you took Willie's and Phil's predictions and reversed them.

Despite the continually poor results, Groundhog Day continues, and folks across North America might be heard reciting one of these poems:

If Groundhog Day is bright and clear
There'll be two winters in the year.
  Or if no shadow do ye see
    An early spring is what there'll be.

Groundhogs, if your aim be true
Then loving fame awaits for you.
But guess ye wrong, and lickety-split:
A groundhog carcass on a stick.

41

If a red sky at night is "a sailor's delight," then what is a red sky in the morning?

Chantal B., Embrun, Ontario

The old saying goes: "Red skies in morning, sailor take warning; red skies at night, sailor's delight." This particular bit of folk wisdom goes back a long way. In the Bible (Matthew 16:2–3), Jesus tells some fishermen that, "When it is evening ye say, it will be fair weather: for the sky is red. And in the morning it will be foul weather today: for the sky is red and lowering."

It would be easy to dismiss this bit of weather folklore but, as it turns out, it actually has a basis in scientific fact. At dusk a red sky indicates that dry weather is on the way. The high-pressure weather system that brings low humidity pushes before it a lot of dust particles, which filter sunlight and make it look red at the horizon. If the evening sky is grey, this means that there are many water droplets in the atmosphere, and they are likely to fall the next day.

Dust at sunrise also causes a red sky in the morning. In this case, however, the dust is being pushed *out* by an approaching low-pressure system bringing in moisture. But don't confuse a red sky in the morning with a red *sun* in the morning. If the sun itself is red and the

Morning! Some red sky up there today!

sky is a normal colour, the day will be fair.

People have depended on observations of nature to forecast changes in the weather for thousands of years. Before there were modern methods of reading weather patterns, it made sense to develop a keen eye for natural signs of weather changes. And even today if you talk to people like farmers, whose jobs depend on the weather, they will often trust their own judgment in observing natural phenomena more than they will the weather office's predictions.

How much does your head weigh?

and Other Bizarre Bits About YOUR BODY

29.

How much does your head weigh?

Christian H., Seattle, Washington

The average human head weighs about 7.5% of a person's body weight. So if you weigh about 40 kilograms, your head weighs around 3 kilos. If you are a 90-kilogram person, your head weighs about 6.75 kilos.

There's a lot in there to make up that mass. Your head has 22 bones — the cranium, which protects the brain, has 8 bones, and the face, 14. So when you get tired of holding your head up high, you know why. It's heavy!

If people never cut their hair, how long would it be when they're 15?

Shirley T., Scarborough, Ontario

Each hair grows from its own follicle. As new cells are produced in the follicles, they push the older cells upward. This is what makes the hair grow. The hair itself is not alive, just the cells in the follicles. New cells are produced for a certain amount of time, depending on where on the body the follicle is located. Then the follicle goes through a rest phase. During this phase the existing hair falls out. When the follicle returns to its active state, a new hair starts to grow in its place. So the maximum length that your hair can grow depends on how long the growth phase is. For most people, scalp hair can keep growing anywhere from two to six years. At any moment, 85% of your head of hair is growing while 15% is resting.

Most hair grows about 1.3 centimetres per month, or 15.6 centimetres a year. (This can vary, depending on your age, your genetics and the state of your hormones.) So do the math: the longest hair you could expect to grow would be about 94 centimetres (6 years x 15.6 cm/year = 93.6 cm).

Hair follicles on different parts of your body are programmed with different growth phases and different rates of growth. Eyelash hairs grow more slowly than scalp hairs, and they grow for only about four months before new hairs replace them.

Some Hairy Facts:

- The palms of your hands, the soles of your feet and your lips are the only places on your body surface where hair doesn't grow.
- There is an average of 100 000 hair follicles on your scalp. Most brunettes have 155 000, blondes 140 000 and redheads only 85 000. On average, you lose up to 125 hairs from your scalp each day.
- You have about 5 million hairs on your body.
- Whether hair is curly or straight depends on the shape of the follicles. Curly hair grows from flat follicles, wavy from oval follicles, and straight from round follicles.
- The longest recorded hair was that of Swami Pandarasannadhi, head of India's Thiruvadu Thurai monastery. His hair was reported in 1949 to be 7.8 metres in length.
- Mata Jagdamba of Ujjain, India, had hair that measured 4.16 metres on February 21, 1994. It was the longest on record, for a person who was alive at the time. But in 1998 that record was broken by two brothers from Northern Thailand. Eighty-five-year-old Hu Saelo, the village shaman, had hair 5.24 metres long. He had not cut it for over 70 years. His brother, Mr. Yi, who had turned 87 in 1997, had hair 4.85 metres long.

31.

When did men start cutting their hair short and why?

Paul J., Toronto, Ontario

Parents' complaints about their kids' hair length and changing hair fashions have been a part of life for much of history. Hair length has gone up and down for centuries because of age, marital and social status, religion, occupation and other reasons. Here's a brief history of hairstyles:

In ancient Egypt, shaved heads and hairless bodies were signs of nobility. The Egyptians even had a barber god, and wealthy men could afford to have barbers come to their homes. As time went on, the Egyptians would wear heavy black wigs for special ceremonies. Sometimes they would also wear false beards.

Barbershops were popular in ancient Greece and Rome. Men would meet to exchange news while they were being shaved or having their hair styled, or having a massage. The most popular hairstyle for Roman men was short, brushed forward and arranged in curls that were made with curling irons — even the older men wore it like this. Men would even use perfume and face paint to beautify themselves.

The Gauls, who lived in what is now France, believed that long hair was a sign of honour. When Julius Caesar conquered them in 50 B.C., he made them cut their hair to demonstrate their submission.

The Bible mentions barbers during the time of Ezekiel. Female barbers have never been as popular as male barbers, maybe because of the story of Samson and Delilah. Samson was an ancient biblical hero who was forbidden to cut his hair, the source of his strength. But the doomed Samson fell in love with a woman named Delilah, who betrayed him to his enemies by cutting off his hair while he slept.

In the Middle Ages longer hair was popular, and most men had beards. Bowl haircuts and the pageboy — where chin-length hair is curled under — were the most popular men's hairstyles. During King Henry VIII's reign, men wore their hair longer and there was more variety in the styles.

In France, cutting off a king's hair was thought to take away his power. But in the sixteenth century, after Francis I of France accidentally burned his hair with a torch, men wore short hair and grew short beards and moustaches. In the seventeenth century upper-class men's hair got longer and wigs gained in popularity. Some of them were extremely tall and curly. Poorer people wore shorter, uncurled haircuts under caps.

Wigs for men were still popular in the eighteenth century in Europe and the American colonies, but they were not as extravagant. The most common style of wig had a ponytail at the back that was either tied with a ribbon or tucked into a bag. For special occasions the wigs were made with white hair or were powdered to be white. Wigs that are still worn by some judges are based on these styles. During the French Revolution in the late 1700s, men returned to more classical Roman hairstyles. In the nineteenth century men kept their hair quite short and seldom wore wigs, but most had some kind of facial hair, either sideburns, beards or moustaches.

During the first half of the twentieth century, most men wore their hair short and were clean-shaven, probably because of the military influence of the First and Second World Wars. In the 1950s Elvis Presley appeared with a shiny black pompadour hairstyle and long sideburns, and in the 1960s The Beatles and other rock-and-roll groups had a big influence on men's hairstyles. Now almost anything goes! No matter how you wear your hair you ought to be able to show your parents that at some point in history it was "all the rage."

- No matter the culture, a person's hairstyle can tell a lot about them:
- Age: In many cultures a child's hair is cut to symbolize that they are entering a new stage of life. In England, young boys would receive their first haircut at about age three — the same time they got their first pair of long pants.
- Marital status: In some African countries a woman's hairstyle shows not only if she's married, but whether or not she has children.
- Occupation: In most cultures, soldiers have the same hairstyle to show their obedience and to signify that they are part of a group.
- Religion: Some religions require that their followers shave or cover their hair, or wear a special hairstyle. Buddhist monks, who believe strongly in having no attachment to material things, keep their heads shaved to avoid distracting themselves from their meditation and prayer.
- Fortune: In Nigeria, children born with thick, curly hair are thought to bring good luck to their parents.
- Reverence: Some tribes in Papua New Guinea believe that your ancestors' spirits live in your hair, so you shouldn't cut it.

Why do so many blond or light-haired men often have darker beards?

Alex W., Waterloo, Ontario

Before we attack the topic of colour, let's look at facial hair in general. Men grow beards for all sorts of reasons: to be fashionable, to be unfashionable, to be a rebel, or to hide behind. (Or maybe because it hurts their skin to shave.) It's important to know that Gillette didn't invent the safety razor until just before World War I. Shaving was much easier after that, and gas masks fit better on a clean-shaven man.

Over the centuries, facial hair has gone in and out of fashion. Back in the second century A.D., Hadrian the emperor grew a beard to conceal some scars, and bingo — Romans copied their emperor. And that's been the pattern: beards have been pretty common, with little surges of popularity when influential men wore one. Today, movie stars rather than emperors often lead the trends.

You have to admit, a beard is one accessory that any man can afford. Sideburns too. They are named after Ambrose Burnsides, an American Civil War general who sported the odd hairline extension. Back in the sixteenth century, there were intriguing descriptive names for beard  styles. The Sugar Loaf was long and rounded, wider at the top than bottom. The Bush, French Fork, Swallow-Tail, Needle, Screw and Fan-Tail all have names that describe them well.

The goatee is a beard with an odd history. When you think about it, representations of the good guys in the Bible (like God, Jesus and Moses) all have big beards like Santa Claus. Yet the devil is usually shown with a goatee. His beard doesn't join up with the sideburns. It's basically a moustache and a goatee (a short pointed beard) that don't meet. It can disguise a disappearing chin, or maybe add sophistication . . . but mostly it makes a man look menacing. Moustaches also seem to have a fairly sinister reputation, as over the years bad guys wore them.

But let's talk colour, finally. The fact is, doctors and scientists don't really know why so many blond or light-haired men have darker, often ruddy beards. (And remember that what you see may not be entirely true, because you have no idea who is dyeing their hair these days.)

Hair and beard colour differences may or may not relate to the apparent age of the follicle. Hair on your head ages first. It gets lighter and thinner and disappears first because the follicle shrinks. Partially that is because of too much time in the sun without a hat. And density seems to decrease from the top down. It's sort of like the places where people go grey first. Most people grey in the area in front of the ear, not behind it or above it. But this doesn't apply to everyone.

• The man sporting the longest recorded beard was Hans Langseth. It measured 5.25 metres when he died in 1927 in Kensett, Iowa. The beard is in the Smithsonian Institute in Washington, D.C.
• Whisker facts: The average man's beard contains 15 500 hairs, which grow 0.038 centimetres each day, or 14 centimetres a year. During his lifetime the average man will spend 3340 hours shaving off 8.4 metres of whiskers. He will shave off nearly half a kilogram of whisker hairs every sixteen years.
• Superb words to toss around are pogonotrophy (beard growing) and pogonotomy (beard cutting).

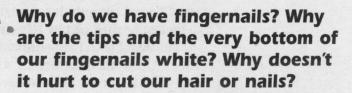

Why does hair change colour as a person gets older?

Jamie, by e-mail

This process is encoded in your genes — you come from your parents programmed for certain things, like which pigment and how much pigment you have in your hair, and when you will go grey. Children's hair colour changes with age. Most "tow headed" white-blond children turn into brunettes because the cells producing that inherited pigment grow and the hair darkens. And the reason your hair goes grey eventually is that cells at the root of the hair, which produce pigment, gradually die off as you age.

And why does our hair get lighter in the summer? When pigments are exposed to sunlight they lose some colour — the way dark-coloured things fade if you leave them in the sun. This mostly happens in the summer when there are so many hours of sunlight. In the winter, indoor lights don't contain the same light energy as sunlight, and won't fade things as fast.

Why do we have fingernails? Why are the tips and the very bottom of our fingernails white? Why doesn't it hurt to cut our hair or nails?

Rajkumar P., Toronto, Ontario

Your fingernails protect the tips of your fingers and your toenails protect the tips of your toes. Fingernails also help you to pick things up (unless you're a nail biter, that is). Most animals have some kind of nails, but they're not always as flat as human nails. Some animals have sharp, curved nails called claws, and others have thicker, rounded nails that we call hooves. Your nails are made of a protein called keratin. That's the same stuff that human hair, bird feathers, horse hooves and bear claws are made of.

The hard part of your nail is dead, and that's why it doesn't hurt to cut your nails or your hair. But the root or flesh part where the nail grows from — your cuticle — is alive. That's why a hangnail hurts so much.

Your fingernails can tell a lot about your health. In order to build protein, you have to have a healthy body. The colour, shape and growth of your nails helps doctors diagnose some illnesses. A really severe illness, like a heart attack or pneumonia, will interrupt growth at the nail root, and doctors will see an indentation across your nail. Other oddities can show lung disease, kidney failure, arsenic poisoning, iron deficiency and even psoriasis. The white tip and whiteness near the root are actually signs of healthy nails.

• Dr. William Bennett Bean, a dermatologist at Cornell University, studied how his nails grew — for 35 years. He found that it takes six months or so for fingernails to grow from the roots to the tip. That's about 3.6 centimetres a year. The longest finger grows nails the fastest, while toenails take up to four times as long. Nails also grow fastest during the day, but grow more slowly as you get older. Nails grow faster on pregnant women, and faster in men than in women.
• Sridhar Chillal of India is in his mid-sixties. He hasn't cut the nails on his left hand in almost 50 years. In 1998 he had a total of almost 6 metres of nails. That includes a 1.4-metre thumbnail and 1.2-metre index fingernail.

Why do armpits smell?

Matt T., Seattle, Washington

First of all, why do we perspire? To keep our bodies cool through evaporation. We have about 3 million sweat glands throughout our bodies! In the summer those glands will pump out between 2 and 2.5 litres of fluid, made up mostly of ammonia and salts. When it is humid the sweat doesn't evaporate, so it just drips off the body without much cooling effect. In dry air we can survive 130°C for up to twenty minutes, but in moist air, 46 – 49°C is the maximum we can tolerate. Why? Because the sweat glands can't work properly in moist conditions.

So that's why we sweat — but not why we smell. Around puberty the apocrine glands (or the human scent glands) start to secrete a pale milky goo that you can't see. You can't even smell it . . . at first. But when the bacteria under your arms have digested it, it starts to stink. It supposedly takes six hours at room temperature for apocrine secretions to develop a noticeable smell. The longer it sits, the stronger the smell.

In 1989 scientists in Philadelphia figured out that the smell of body odour is a chemical called 3-methyl-2-hexenoic acid. How they figured this out is the best part. They had volunteers go for a week without bathing. The volunteers washed just once with non-deodorant soap, then walked around with cotton pads under their armpits for a week. Then scientists used a gas chromatography machine to isolate each chemical in the sweat, and they got in some odour experts to sniff each one. The culprit for the unpleasant odour was 3-methyl-2-hexenoic acid.

We need to remember that much of our displeasure with this smell is cultural. Back in the 1880s the novelist Joris-Karl Huysmans thought the aroma was pretty great. He celebrated armpits as a gift of nature, calling them "spice boxes" that "season and enhance the dew of love."

The Elizabethans were keen on natural smells too. Elizabethan women actually gave their sweethearts a "Love Apple" to treasure as a token of affection. The recipe called for stowing a peeled apple in the armpit until well seasoned, and then passing it on to the love of one's life. (It is doubtful that this custom will make a comeback.)

A research lab in Cincinnati actually tests deodorant effectiveness for manufacturers. These people are odour judges, and they've been in the business for a long time. The odour judges insist that gender, weight, body type and hairiness have little to do with underarm odour — and they've sniffed thousands of underarms. These experts say odour is mostly a combination of body chemistry, how active your apocrine glands are, and the types of bacteria living in your armpits. However, the bit about no difference between genders is much debated. Some dermatologists insist that men smell more because their apocrine gland is driven by male hormones called androgens. The poet Catullus wrote about the "fierce goat" beneath a man's arms. Asian men are the exception. They have few apocrine glands, and just don't sweat much.

So here's the bottom line: How do you combat 3-methyl-2-hexenoic acid or "B.O."? You have two choices: use deodorant or antiperspirant-deodorant. A deodorant kills bacteria and is usually scented — partly to mask odours, but mostly because the market is "fragrance driven." But to stay dry you need an antiperspirant-deodorant. It kills bacteria too, but works chiefly by making armpits a dryer and less hospitable place for bacteria, by stopping up the openings of the sweat glands. It's an odd idea, but it works.

What is the point of hiccups?

Kevin T., Seattle, Washington

The medical term for hiccups is singultus. You hiccup when your diaphragm gets out of sync with the other breathing muscles. Your diaphragm is a large, flat muscle that lies just under your rib cage. It stretches across your abdomen, from your belly to your back, and works by pumping up and down to move air into and out of the lungs. It pulls down when you inhale, to help pull air into the lungs, and pushes up when you exhale, to help push air out. If it pumps too fast, you get hiccups. The diaphragm sends a gust of air rushing into your lungs, and your brain tells your tongue and the opening to your throat to clamp down to stop the flow of air. This clamping shut makes the air rush across your voice box, creating the hiccup sound. Anything that causes your stomach to stretch suddenly can set off a case of hiccups — gulping down a meal, or swallowing too much air when you're laughing or crying, are common causes.

But what's the *point* of hiccups? There isn't one, really. They're simply an effect of your diaphragm pumping too fast.

• If hiccups last for more than a day or two, you should go to your doctor, but usually they stop on their own. There are lots of folk remedies for getting rid of them. Some of the weirder ones suggest that you:
• drink 9 swallows of water from your grandfather's cup without taking a breath
• wet a piece of red thread with your tongue, stick the thread on your forehead and try to look at it.

Why does your stomach "growl" when you are hungry?

Rebecca L., by e-mail

"Why" isn't all that thrilling — rumbling or growling is just a normal part of digestion. As foods and digestive juices move on down the digestive tract, your stomach might rumble. That's the sound of stomach muscles contracting and pushing the stomach contents through a valve called the pylorus. This happens even more often when your stomach has gone a few hours without adding food. What is thrilling is the term for this growling: borborygmus. If you find stomach rumbling embarrassing, you can eat smaller meals more often so your stomach is never completely empty. Or, you can just go with it, and declare, "Hey, judging from this borborygmus I would say it's time to eat!"

We eat and drink things that are many different colours. Why do they all come out the other end brown?

Peter and David C., Toronto, Ontario

The saying "garbage in, garbage out" doesn't really apply here. You eat good food and it comes out the other end as something you need to flush away. Waste is simply a fact of life. And your own waste is brown because of something that happens in the gut (or intestine) on the way out.

In fact, it is not just your digested food you see in the toilet bowl. Your blood is constantly re-building itself, and the blood cells your body is done with also need to be flushed out of your system. To leave your system those cells first need to break down, and when they decompose one of the components is a chemical called bilirubin. And guess what colour it is? Brown. Bingo.

And what about the colour of another bodily waste, urine? Urine is 95% water, and includes mineral salts, toxins, ammonia, urea and uric acid. It also contains the yellow pigment, urochrome, which is part of the breakdown of blood.

39. Is there really such a thing as phantom pain?

Alex M., Vancouver, B.C.

A phantom sensation or phantom pain happens to a person who has had a part of his or her body amputated, but can still feel where that body part used to be. It can be tingling, a feeling of warmth or cold, cramps, constriction, or mild to severe pain. Almost all amputees have experienced some kind of phantom sensations, but every person is different. A few may never have any phantom sensations, but some amputees have severe phantom pains for years. These are usually worst in the first year after amputation, but they can last for many years.

No one knows exactly what causes phantom pain. According to one theory, the thalamus — a part of the brain — is still sending messages through the nerves to the limb that is no longer there, causing a pain or sensation that feels as if the limb *is* still there. Some children born without a limb have said they can feel the body part, even though it has never been there.

Why is it called chicken pox?

Jacob Hiatt Magnet School, Worcester, Massachusetts

This is a great question, because the answer is absolutely not what you would expect.

It seems that when chicken pox was first noticed, the medical people of the time thought that the spots or blisters were stuck on the skin — when in fact the skin erupts into the rash. The stuck-on-the-skin school thought the spots looked like garbanzo beans attached all over the body. The Latin word for garbanzo beans is *cicer*— thus their more common English name, chick peas. And from that we get chick[en] pox. If the Spanish term, garbanzo beans, had been more popular, we might be using the term garbanzo pox today!

So likely the source of the term chicken pox is not about the animal — chicken — it's about the vegetable — chick peas.

One other theory is that this common illness might have been called chicken pox because it's less serious than smallpox, and the term "chicken" suggested that it wasn't so dangerous.

How come if one person yawns, another person does it right afterwards?

Kelly M., Sayville, New York

The jury's still out on that one. In fact, scientists don't really know why we yawn. They will go as far as to admit that a yawn is a slow breath. Some think we yawn because we are bored or tired. Watch a cat or a dog — they seem to yawn more when they are bored.

Some people think we yawn when there isn't enough air in the room. We also yawn when we are falling asleep and when we wake up. The theory is that at those times our breathing is shallow, and a yawn gives us a fresh lungful of air. But other scientists think that theory is nonsense. They have put yawners into rooms full of oxygen . . . and they yawned anyway. Some think we yawn to stretch our neck muscles; others think we yawn to get more oxygen into the bloodstream. The theory is that yawning helps the body work better by stretching the breathing muscles.

Although we all think that yawning is contagious — if we see someone yawning we will likely yawn too — some scientists say it is not. They believe it is something that you can talk yourself out of doing, and that if it really was contagious you couldn't talk yourself out of it.

During the Middle Ages, long before scientists tackled this problem, people thought that the devil made them yawn. If you succumbed to that uncontrollable urge to yawn, the devil could enter your soul through your mouth. And if he didn't make it the first time, he would make you yawn again so he could try again. People in those times would make the sign of the cross when they felt a yawn coming on, to defend against the devil.

We don't believe that anymore, but everything scientists have to say about yawning doesn't answer the question either. The theory that fits best has to do with contagious yawning being a social function. Maybe we get this contagious yawning thing from our evolutionary ancestors, the apes and chimpanzees. Hang around a zoo and you will find that apes also have infectious yawns. One starts and the whole gang yawns too. Mike Meredith of the Neuroscience Program at Florida State University figures that this common action might bind the troop together. "The sight or sound of a yawn . . . does tend to start everyone yawning," he says. "I don't know if it ever functions as a signal for everyone to find a place to sleep for the night. There would be some advantage to such a signal because ape troops gain safety by sticking together, as people do."

But the bottom line is that these are all simply theories, and just thinking about yawning can make you do it — like right now.

Why does poison ivy itch so much? Why do some people catch it, and some don't?

Dave, by e-mail

We aren't talking about the Batman character, Poison Ivy. We're talking about a common plant. The oil in the sap of poison ivy, urushiol, puts the "poison" in the poison ivy. And get this: you only need a billionth of a gram (a nanogram) to get a rash and itch like mad. Five hundred people could itch from the amount covering the head of a pin. If you could pull together just over 7 grams of urushiol, you could give every person on earth a rash. Even dead plants contain active urushiol.

Not absolutely everyone reacts to poison ivy, but most people do. It's the most common allergy. And even if you don't react the first time you have contact with it, you might after another exposure. You don't even have to see a plant to get a reaction — your shoes or pants might have rubbed onto the plants, and when you touch them, bingo . . . allergic contact dermatitis. In other words, a nasty rash. Or maybe your dog or cat has walked through poison ivy and you give them a nice pat . . . Ouch.

The old saying is "leaves of three, leave it be." So if you see this plant with its set of three distinct leaves, leave it alone! What can you do if you *do* come into contact with poison ivy? Whatever you do, don't touch or scratch your skin, at least until you can wash it. Wash your hands, the affected area, then your hands again. Cold water closes your pores to the urushiol oil. If you can avoid touching or scratching the area, you have a better chance of avoiding a rash.

A plant called jewel weed — which handily often grows alongside poison ivy — is a good remedy. Grab some and crush the leaves and stems to get the juice out, then rub it all over where you were exposed to the poison ivy. It should slow down the itching and spreading. Experts on this believe jewel weed to be superior to the medicines available. (Make sure you use the right plant, though. Jewel weed has oval leaves with round-toothed edges. Its yellow-orange, trumpet-like flowers have dark red spots. You can also buy jewel weed soap and sprays.)

Unfortunately, even after using jewel weed, you aren't "out of the woods" yet, because as your rash heals you have to stop yourself from scratching it. Make a thick paste of baking soda and water, and plaster it on to help with the itching. All in all, this is nasty business, so avoid it if you can.

What is Prince William's favourite colour?

and Other UNUSUAL BUT USEFUL INFORMATION

What is Prince William's favourite colour?

They don't call Prince William "His Royal Shyness" (okay, it's "Sighness") for nothing. Considering the amount of exposure he's had — books, magazine and newspaper articles, television coverage and Web sites — we know very little about him. He rarely speaks to the press. We do know that:

- His favourite foods are mostly fast foods.
- He likes techno and classical music.
- He likes school, computer games, reading action adventures and non-fiction, and watching action movies.
- He was born June 21, 1982 at 9:03 p.m. at St. Mary's Hospital in Paddington, London, which makes his birth sign Cancer. Weight at birth: 3.43 kilograms.
- His royal title is His Royal Highness Prince William of Wales. When he was born it took a few days for his parents to name him, so he was referred to as the Prince of Wails.
- His full name is William Arthur Philip Louis Mountbatten Windsor. His actual last name should be Schlesweig-Holstein-Sonderburg-Glucksburg-Saxe-Coburg-Gotha. However, the Queen decreed that royal descendants would take the name Windsor.
- Nicknames: Wills, Willy Wombat, His Naughtiness, William the Terrible, Billy the Basher and — more recently — Dreamboat Willy and His Royal Sighness.
- He is second in line to the throne of England, after his father, Prince Charles.
- He has a female Black Labrador called Widgeon.
- And, last but not least, blue and dark green are his fave colours.

What if someone was born on February 29? Would they be a year old in four years, or do they celebrate their birthday on March 1?

Jackie N., San Jose, California

It seems that if you are a "leap day" baby, things could go a few different ways for you. Likely, your pals and brothers and sisters will tease you about not having a birthday three out of four years. But it can work in your favour, since leap day babies still tend to celebrate their birthdays, but on either February 28 or March 1. When there *is* a leap year they have a major blowout on February 29.

But why do we have a leap year at all? It's about leftovers — leftover time, to be exact. It takes a day for the earth to spin once on its axis. And it takes a year to go around the sun. Actually, 365 days, 5 hours, 48 minutes and 45 seconds. Julius Caesar decided that a correction was needed, so every four years we add one day to our year to use up these extra minutes — that's where the leap day comes in.

Knowing this, you can figure out that you have a 1 in 1461 (365 + 365 + 365 + 366) chance of being a leap day baby. And if you are, here's how to figure out if this is your year: You get a birthday if the year is divisible by 4, and not divisible by 100 unless it is also divisible by 400. So 2000 is a leap year, but 1900 wasn't. 2004 will be too. For more info, check out the leap year Web site (see page 155).

But February 29 has special significance even if you weren't born that day. It's also known as Sadie Hawkins' Day, the day when women can propose marriage to men. In former times, it was always the man who proposed to the woman, or to her parents.

For at least four hundred years, apparently, European folk custom has said that a woman may propose marriage in a leap year. If the man should refuse the offer, he has to give a consolation prize of a silk gown.

Where did that idea come from? There are a few theories. The best one is the legend that St. Patrick originated the custom back in the fifth century, when both priests and nuns were allowed to marry. On behalf of her fellow nuns, the powerful abbess St. Bridget complained to St. Patrick that the nuns could not pop the question to *their* admirers. The two saints arrived at a compromise, whereby every fourth year the *sisters* would have the chance to propose. (Patrick refused the offer, but gave Bridget the gown.)

So that's the notion for this turnaround in the male-female roles, but that doesn't explain about Sadie Hawkins or about February 29 specifically.

Sadie Hawkins was a cartoon character in a strip called "L'il Abner" by Al Capp. She was the daughter of Dogpatch mayor Hekzebiah Hawkins. Sadie was unmarried, so to find her a husband, her father gathered a group of bachelors together, then got them to start running. Moments later, Sadie set out after them, caught a man, and married him. The other unmarried Dogpatch women thought it was such a great plan that Sadie Hawkins' Day became an annual event. Colleges and high schools in the U.S. picked up the idea after the strip ran in 1937, and started having Sadie Hawkins' dances (and dressing up as hillbillies), around the first Saturday after November 11, the day appointed by Mayor Hawkins.

Eventually, St. Patrick's fifth-century custom got mixed in with Al Capp's cartoon spinoff, and February 29 — the day women could propose to men — ended up as Sadie Hawkins' Day, even though it probably *ought* to be called St. Bridget's Day.

And about your age if you're a leap year baby? There's no law, so you can say whatever you want, that you're turning 3 or 12.

What is the typical amount of water it takes to put out a house fire?

Greg M., by e-mail

It turns out that this is a question that highly skilled practitioners and engineers in the fire industry have spent years trying to figure out. There is no typical amount of water, because there is no typical fire. According to John Vokes, Director of the Fire and Safety Division of the Justice Institute of B.C., fires vary depending on a number of factors:

• what the house is made of, and its design

• how long the fire was burning — and how hot it got — before someone started trying to put it out

• how much oxygen (needed for the burning process) is getting to the fire

• the flammability of material on walls, floor and ceiling

• whether there are things like residential sprinklers at work

• the presence and flammability of fuel and other materials near the fire

• the method of and type of equipment used to apply water to the fire

To put it another way, it may take under 10 litres of water to extinguish a small fire in a 108-square-metre house if the firefighters catch it after only two minutes of burning. But it might take close to 10 000 litres to extinguish the fire if it is allowed to burn in the same house for 20 minutes.

Of course the question of how much water is needed to extinguish a fire is particularly important to rural communities with volunteer fire departments, where the response time tends to be longer, than in urban areas, where response times are generally shorter.

46.

What is the world's circumference?

Gael, by e-mail

The first person to figure out the circumference of the earth was Eratosthenes (276–195 B.C.). He was a Greek mathematician and scholar who ran the Great Library at Alexandria. Today he is known as the "father of geography."

Here is the amazing way he figured out the calculation. Eratosthenes read about a deep well in Cyrene (now called Aswan) in southern Egypt, a well that was entirely lit up by the sun at noon, just once a year. He knew that this would only happen when the sun was directly overhead. He also knew that on the day when this happened in Cyrene, the sun was not directly overhead at the same time in Alexandria, because at that exact time in Alexandria, vertical objects cast a shadow. So at the time that the well in Cyrene was completely lit, Eratosthenes measured the shadow cast by a pole in Alexandria. Using his knowledge of geometry, and knowing the distance between Alexandria and Cyrene, he determined that the circumference of the earth was 250 000 *stadia*. (A *stadion* was the commonly used measure of length in the ancient world. Professional pacers were hired to walk from one place to another while counting their steps.) Eratosthenes's calculation translates to about 40 000 kilometres — a figure that's remarkably close to the earth's actual circumference at the equator, which we now know is 39 842 kilometres.

Why did people bind their feet?

Natalie L., Mt. Vernon, Illinois

The Chinese custom of binding feet — where the mother, sister or nurse of a girl aged three to five would wrap her feet tightly so they wouldn't grow normally — was around for about 1000 years. A 3-metre-long bandage was used to wrap the foot tightly, bending the toes over and breaking the bones, eventually forcing the ball of the foot closer to the heel. Over time the toes were permanently bent in toward the foot. In the era of foot binding, it was desirable to have feet that were shorter than 10 centimetres when full-grown. These tiny feet were called "golden lotus" or "lily feet."

Binding made a girl more "valuable" as a wife because such tiny feet were thought to be dainty, elegant and a sign of good breeding — much the same way that the wearing of tight, confining corsets by Western women from the 1500s to the 1900s was thought to be elegant and attractive. Many poor people did not bind their daughters' feet because they could not afford to have women who could not walk and do work.

There are a couple of stories about how this custom started in China. One is that it began in the eleventh century when the Emperor's daughter was born with deformed feet. To be sure that the girl would not be embarrassed, the Emperor decreed that only women with small feet were desirable. As a result, women began to bind their feet to make them as small as possible. The other story is that it started in the tenth century when girls wanted to imitate the Emperor's concubine (his second wife), who was required to dance with her feet bound.

Either way, having bound feet meant that the girl would have a lot of trouble walking. She would have to take very tiny steps, and often needed to have a servant or a cane to help her keep her balance. The gait of girls with bound feet was called the "willow walk." Often women with bound feet were confined to their homes, since walking was so painful.

Special shoes called "lotus slippers" had soft soles and a soft padded upper that covered the whole foot. Women spent hours embroidering the slippers, and they were kept spotlessly clean and were often perfumed — partly because bound feet stank under all those wrappings. You can see these slippers in many museum collections.

The practice of foot binding was officially banned in 1911, but it carried on for a number of years after that. There are still a few very elderly women living who have bound feet.

Cinderella!
Where's that
shoehorn?

Why are the keys on the keyboard not in alphabetical order?

Joel A., Prince Albert, Saskatchewan

If you've only ever used a computer, this will take some imagination. The first keyboards were on typewriters. They were designed so that each letter was on the end of a separate bar of metal. As you hit the key, the metal bar swung forward and hit the sheet of paper, placing the inked letter where you wanted it.

The first keyboards were arranged in a logical way —alphabetically. However, we use some letters more than others. Often-used letters close to each other would jam each time their swinging bars collided. No one could pick up any speed, making typing a very frustrating process.

Christopher Sholes patented what is close to the current typewriter in 1868. (The first recorded patent for a typewriter was granted to Henry Mill, a British Engineer, in 1714, but it was nowhere near as practical as Sholes' design.) In 1872 Sholes went back to the drawing board. He figured out which letters were used the most, and rearranged the sequence on the keyboard. His goal was to make sure that when you typed *ing* or *th* or any of the other common combinations of letters, the keys would be spread out in such a way that the metal bars would never jam. What he came up with is called the QWERTY keyboard, after the six letters in the top row, starting at the left.

It took a while for typists to catch on to the QWERTY keyboard, but it is the standard even today. There has been one significant attempt to replace the QWERTY keyboard. The Dvorak, named after August Dvorak, who taught education at the University of Washington, was invented in 1936.

Dvorak decided that the middle row should contain the vowels for the left hand (*a, e, i, o, u*) and the most frequently used consonants for the right hand (*d, h, t, n, s*). He thought his set-up let typists go faster, but people complained that it was too much trouble to learn something new.

The QWERTY keyboard is pretty much the only part of a typewriter that is also part of a computer. We've come along way since 1872.

- Mark Twain (who wrote *Tom Sawyer*) bought one of the earliest typewriters. He was the first American author to deliver a typewritten manuscript to a publisher: *Life on the Mississippi*.
- Using only the top row of the keyboard, you can type the word TYPEWRITER. Here are some more top row words: PREREQUIRE, PROPRIETOR, REPERTOIRE, REPETITORY and PERPETUITY.
- The longest word which can be typed using only the fingers of the left hand is: AFTERCATARACTS. Slightly shorter words are: STEWARDESSES and REVERBERATED.
- The longest words which can be typed using only the fingers of the right hand are JOHNNY JUMP-UP, LOLLIPOP, POLYPHONY, NIMINY-PIMINY and HYPOPHYLLIUM.
- The longest word which can be typed using only the middle row is ALFALFAS.
- The following sentence uses every letter of the alphabet: "The quick brown fox jumps over the lazy dog."
- The letters used most often, in order, are: *e, t, o* and *s*.
- The letters used least often are: *h, j, x, z* and *q*.

How were candy canes invented?

and Other Festive Facts About HOLIDAYS

49.

How were candy canes invented?

Katrina A., by e-mail

Like all good (and tasty) traditions, this one comes with a host of plausible stories. Which one is true is up to you. What is a candy cane? A white peppermint stick striped with red in the shape of a cane . . . or is it the shape of shepherd's crook? There's a legend about a candymaker running out of room on his baking pans, and bending the candy sticks out of necessity. There is another story that someone thought they should be able to hang up the candy sticks on the tree. Hence the crook. And since it is Christmas candy, maybe it is the shape of a J, for Jesus.

Spangler Candy Company in Ohio makes 2.5 million candy canes a day. They say that candy canes date back to Germany 350 years ago. The candy started out as plain white sugar sticks used to pacify babies, and apparently to reward kids who sang in church choirs. The story goes that the choir master at a cathedral back in the 1600s came up with the idea to shape the sticks into crooks like the ones the shepherds carried at the time of Jesus' birth. He did it to keep the boys in the choir quiet during the long Nativity ceremony. A brilliant idea.

Eventually the smaller sugar crooks became Christmas tree decorations. Around the early 1900s the red stripe was added, and peppermint flavouring too. Small candy stores handmade them for their customers, and by the 1950s large candy companies mechanized the process of producing hard-pulled sugar candy into cane shapes. Now we see them everywhere.

50.

Who got the idea of having Christmas trees, and what does holly have to do with Christmas?

Lisa B., Montgomery, New Jersey, and Brooke W., Annville, Pennsylvania, by e-mail

December 25 worked out nicely as a Christian festival to celebrate a new life, because a number of pagan festivals honouring a similar thing already existed for that time of the year. The Romans honoured their god Saturn between December 17 and 23, at the *Saturnalia*. It was the time of the winter solstice and of celebrating the fact that after the shortest day comes the rebirth of light. On January 1, along with a new year's feast, there was *Juvenalia*, the festival of childhood and youth. Add to that the Jewish festival of lights, (Chanukah or Hanukka, which takes place in December), Yule (a Baltic and Scandinavian winter festival in honour of the gods Odin and Thor), and *Sacaea* (a Middle Eastern festival to welcome the new year). You can see that there were already a number of customs involving gift exchanges, game playing, eating and general merriment, before Christmas celebrations became common.

The Christians went in for decorations too. But why the shiny green prickly-leafed holly bush, or Christmas trees? It's a big and serious reason: they are *ever* — as in, always — *green*, and so are seen as symbols of life in the dark of winter. The Romans had had these life symbols too, and Christians incorporated the use of evergreens into their beliefs of everlasting life.

Holly has been a popular winter decoration for thousands of years. The Romans had a custom of bringing evergreens to people during winter celebrations, because evergreens meant good luck.

Before Christianity, holly was a pagan symbol of immortality. In ancient times holly was thought to protect your house and bring you good luck and long life. The Romans thought that the prickles would stab and repel witches, demons and evil spirits.

The Christians considered the prickles to be like the crown of thorns that Christ wore at his crucifixion, so the holly's festive red berries came to represent the drops of blood where the thorns had pierced Christ's flesh. (In Denmark, holly is known as Christ-thorn.)

There were also lots of superstitions and beliefs about hanging holly:
- Holly was considered to represent the male and ivy the female. Because holly was the male symbol, only men could bring it into the house.
- If you nailed up a sprig in the cowshed, your beasts would thrive.
- A berried sprig was the ideal ornament for the top of the Christmas pudding, and a scrap was preserved and burned under next year's plum pudding, as a charm for continuity.

What about Christmas trees? Trees were originally decorated as a peace offering to the spirits who supposedly took off with the leaves in the winter. People would drape the bare branches with painted cloth and coloured stones, and what do you know, it worked! The leaves came back in the spring!

The Germans first erected trees at Christmas, and covered them with decorations lit with candles. The first Christmas trees were oaks, because early German pagans were keen on them — in fact, they worshipped the mighty oak. As was often the case, rather than trying to ban a custom, the Christian missionaries adopted the idea. But Christians went for the fir because of its triangular shape. The triangle is the sign of the holy Trinity (the Father, Son and Holy Spirit).

51.

How did the tradition of giving gifts on Christmas start?

Liz, Toronto, Ontario

You'd expect the answer would be because of the three wise men offering gifts to the infant Christ — but gift-giving goes back way before that. A gift exchange is an ancient midwinter custom. It goes back to the stone age, 10 000 years ago, when the practice of farming was widespread enough that there was a slight food surplus. Extra food would be put into storage and brought out daily, and when the halfway point was reached at midwinter, they knew they were going to make it through the long cold season. They could relax, so they had a celebration.

Each farmer had his own specialty, or what he grew best, so there was a big food exchange along with the feast. Sort of like a potluck dinner, with doggie bags. Or similar to the potlatch tradition of the Northwest Coast Indians, where they re-distribute wealth. And as the centuries rolled on — but still before Christianity — the gift-giving got more involved. In ancient Rome the ceremonies at winter solstice, *Saturnalia*, got very elaborate. Popular gifts were honey, fruit, lamps and gold coins. Failure to give presents was said to bring extremely bad luck.

The early Christians apparently tried to end this pagan gift-giving ritual, but people weren't keen on letting it go. They made it a sacred thing instead. Gift-giving would symbolize Christ's birth as well as the gifts from the wise men. It fitted with the Christian ideal of unselfishness in giving to the poor and the needy too, so the gift swap continued.

The rather lavish gift exchange we see today began around the same time as the modern Santa. It was all part of the nineteenth-century commercialization of Christmas. Along with that came the wrapping of presents. Handmade presents were the norm at first, but around 1900, people started to give store-bought, manufactured gifts. They were convenient, but less personal than handmade gifts, so to give them the personal touch, retailers encouraged shoppers to have their purchases gift-wrapped.

People often say jokingly that Christmas cards and wrapping paper were a Hallmark Cards Company invention. That's not quite true . . . but it's close. The first creator of a commercial Christmas card was John Calcott Horsley, an English artist who sold his first work in 1843. It was a drawing of a family sitting down to a feast, and it said "Merry Christmas and a Happy New Year to you." Cards became very popular in the U.S. when lithographer Louis Prang set up business in Boston in the 1870s.

Enter Joyce Hall, a boy from Nebraska who went to Kansas City in 1910 to sell picture postcards. Hall developed a system for distributing to dealers — an idea that was an innovation at the time. Within four years he gave up postcards and went into greeting cards, with a special focus on Christmas cards. Hallmark Cards was born. Norman Rockwell created Hallmark's most famous Christmas cards, but over the years Hallmark bought designs from other famous artists. Today the company prints about 11 million cards every day.

The first thing Hallmark added to their line of cards was special gift-wrapping paper. During the Christmas rush in 1917 they ran out of tissue wrapping paper, so they tried selling some old envelope-lining papers from their warehouse, at 10¢ a sheet. Customers went wild, so they began manufacturing all kinds of designs . . . and there's been no turning back.

Why do kids hunt for Easter eggs at Easter?

Devin C., Massapequa, New York

In almost every culture there is some sort of celebration of the arrival of spring, and for thousands of years the egg has played its part as a symbol of life. The ancient Greeks, Romans, Egyptians, Persians and Chinese gave eggs as gifts during the spring rituals. The egg stands for the universe and new life, and was believed to have special powers. Early Christians saw it as a symbol of the resurrection of Jesus and the rebirth of man, so the egg became part of Easter celebrations.

There's a Polish legend that tells of Mary giving eggs to the soldiers at the cross when Jesus was crucified. As she wept, her tears fell on the eggs and spotted them with dots of brilliant colour. Another Polish legend says that when Mary Magdalene went to take care of the body of Jesus, she carried a basket of eggs for her meal. When she uncovered the basket, the white eggs had turned the colours of the rainbow.

Egg decoration has all sorts of variations. Greeks dye the eggs crimson red to symbolize the blood of Christ. Slavic people like Russians, Ukrainians and Poles decorate their eggs with elaborate patterns. These are called *pysanki* eggs. Some of the designs have special meanings, and are handed down in a family from generation to generation. In England people would write messages and dates on the eggs they gave as gifts. In the 1800s candy eggs started to be given instead of real eggs. Some were very elaborate, with windows and tiny scenes inside.

The goldsmith Peter Carl Fabergé made the most famous Easter eggs. Russian Czar Alexander III gave his wife, Marie Feodorovna, the first Fabergé egg in 1886 as an Easter gift. It was made of platinum, and opened to reveal a smaller golden egg inside. The smaller golden egg opened to display a golden chicken and a miniature version of the Imperial crown. The tradition of giving an "Imperial Egg" continued for the next three decades — every year there was great anticipation to see what design Fabergé had come up with. Each egg was more magnificent than the last.

• The world's largest Easter egg is in Vegreville, a small Ukrainian town in Alberta. Built in 1975, it's decorated in traditional Ukrainian style. It is 9 metres tall, and took 12 000 hours to design and build.

• On Easter Monday, families gather in Washington, D.C., for the Easter Monday Egg Roll. The egg roll started in the 1870s and has been cancelled only a few times, because of poor weather and during World Wars I and II. Children gather on the lawn of the White House and roll hard-boiled eggs across the lawn. Each egg roller receives a special wooden egg with the signatures of the President and the First Lady.

Why is a bunny connected with Easter?

Aaron N., Appleton, Wisconsin

If you've ever kept rabbits, you'll know that they can produce lots of babies in a short amount of time. The rabbit has been a symbol of birth and new life during the spring season for thousands of years.

The Easter bunny tradition seems to have started in Germany — there it's called *Oschter Haws*. There are writings about it from as far back as the 1500s. One legend tells about a poor woman who had no food and no gifts for her children at Easter, so she dyed some eggs and hid them in a nest. The next morning when the children went hunting for the eggs, a big rabbit leapt out of the nest and hopped away. The story spread that the rabbit had brought the Easter eggs for the children. German immigrants brought the Easter bunny idea to America in the 1700s.

Children would build nests out in the gardens around their homes and wait for the Easter bunny to come and lay its coloured eggs. This is where Easter egg hunts — that other Easter tradition — come from.

In 1989 the Eveready Battery Company brought us one of the most popular rabbits around today, the Energizer Bunny. This famous pink bunny got his start in a series of television commercials that use the slogan "keeps going and going and going." It's been one of the most popular ad campaigns of all time. Now you can buy Energizer Bunny stuffed toys, mechanical toys, T-shirts and even screen savers for your computer.

54.

On Hallowe'en some children call out, "Shell out, shell out, the witches are out." How common is this? What else do kids say?

Donald C., Palmerston North, New Zealand

First let's get this tradition sorted out. The Hallowe'en we celebrate is the result of a big witches' brew of traditions that has been stirred up over the ages. The earliest Hallowe'en was in fact a big Druid festival named for the Lord of the Dead, Samhain. (It was the end of the Celtic year, and Samhain means "summer's end.") Folks dressed up in the masks of animals, and at the end of the festivities was the original Hallowe'en bonfire. But in those days, the Druids burned criminals too, with the idea that they were warding off evil spirits.

The conquering Romans hated this and every other Druid custom, so they came up with their own fall festivals, but the bonfire part carried on. The Christians condemned Samhain as well, but folks still continued to keep up bits of it. Eventually, in 835, Pope Gregory IV made a sort of compromise. He moved a May celebration called All Saints' Day or All Hallows' Day to November 1, figuring this would make the day more religious and prayer-filled. But old habits die hard. The festivals continued on the night before November 1 — October 31, or All Hallows' Eve. The name was eventually contracted to Hallowe'en.

It was a scary and superstitious night, so farmers in the British Isles would carry torches to frighten away witches. Irish children carried candle-lit lanterns made from turnips, to protect them from evil spirits. (Their "o'lanterns" were the forerunner of today's Jack-o'-lantern. (The Jack part of the word involves a long tale about a fellow who lost his soul to the devil, who then let him light his way to hell with a coal stuffed into the turnip he had been eating.)

And then there were — and still are — Guy Fawkes celebrations on November 5. Children would dress up a dummy as a historical rebel named Guy Fawkes and beg "a penny for the guy" from strangers. (His name is where our word "guy" comes from.) There is a related Irish custom of soliciting contributions in the name of Muck Olla on the Eve of Samhain. Muck Olla was a shadowy figure who would be sure to wreak vengeance on the selfish. Eventually, his vengeance turned into the wrath of goblins. Disappointed (treat-less) humans might just come up with a few pranks and tricks of their own — and that's how we got the idea of trick or treat.

The tradition of children parading around in costumes is a twentieth-century addition. However, it too may have evolved from some older customs. On All Souls' Day (November 2), costumed children used to go door-to-door, offering to pray or fast for the dead in exchange for money or gifts. There are parts of England where people would hand out small cakes called "soul cakes" to the petitioners, and in Yorkshire it was even called "Cake Night." Carollers would travel from house to house on Cake Night singing:

Soul! Soul! for a soul cake!
I pray, good missus, a soul cake!
An apple or pear, a plum or cherry,
Any good thing to make us merry,
One for Peter, two for Paul,
Three for Him who made us all.

So what about Hallowe'en hollers? In many places children call "trick or treat." Some believe that you have to give the little ghosts and goblins a treat, or they will perform a trick on you. And in other places adults ask children to perform a trick to earn their treat. Other calls include "Hallowe'en apples" and "Shell out, shell out, the witches are out," but "Shell out" seems to have mostly died out about 40 years ago. In the prairies in the 1950s, kids used to say "Apples, nuts or candy, or over goes your shanty." (They meant they'd tip over the outhouse.) That one can't exactly be used today, in most parts of the country. Nowadays kids also say "Trick or treat, smell my feet, give me something good to eat!"

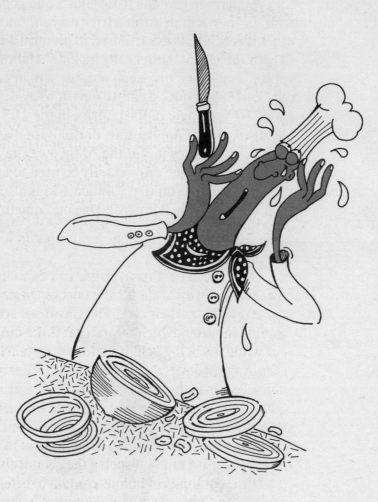

Why do you cry when you cut an onion?

and Other Fascinating Facts About FOOD

Why do you cry when you cut an onion?

The WHALE group at Cozy Harbor Children's Center, North East, Maryland

It's actually a very long story, but basically people cry because cutting the onion releases enzymes that mix with other molecules, converting the sulphur compounds in the onion to molecules that produce strong smells. The body reacts by producing tears to keep the nasty chemicals away from the eyes. The conversion takes about 30 seconds from the time the onion is first cut, and the whole thing is over in about 5 minutes (unless another onion is cut!).

There are a few things people can do to make sure not as many of the stinky burning molecules make it as far as their eyes. The chemicals are soluble in water, which means that if the onion is cut while it's being held it under water, most of the chemicals go down the drain. That way, not as much gets into the air to drive people's eyes crazy. Other good ideas are to heat or freeze the onion to slow down the reaction between the sulphur compound and the enzyme, to chop them in a breeze, or use a fan to disperse the chemicals.

Different kinds of onions contain a different amount and type of sulphur. Some are harsher and some are milder, so people can pick their onion according to their tolerance level. It's worth the tears, since onions taste great, have lots of nutrients (including vitamins B, C and G), and have many other great characteristics such as anti-inflammatory, anti-allergic and anti-asthmatic properties.

56.

What is the record for the heaviest watermelon? And how big was the biggest pizza? Who decides? And how do you prove it?

M.K.W., Somerset County, New Jersey,
and N. Soloway, Creston, B.C.

If you think you have accomplished something extraordinary, you might want to talk to the folks at Guinness World Records. Biggest, smallest, tallest, heaviest, weirdest . . . Then there's the collection of the largest, the youngest, the oldest . . . You name the superlative, Guinness is interested. Read the latest *Guinness Book of World Records* to get the idea. It comes out every year. Break a record and you can get in the book and receive a certificate.

But you have to prove you've broken a record. You can do that by sending in a labelled VHS videocassette of your feat (and if it is a timed event, make sure the clock shows in the film). You should send in good colour photos too. If a local newspaper covers your event, send in the clippings. Then you have to document your claim. (You need at least two independent witness statements by a person of community standing — such as a doctor, a lawyer, a police officer or a professional sports official.) You can't be related to the witness. This all helps the committees at Guinness decide if you really have achieved what you say you have.

Most of the hundreds of categories have guidelines, so it is best to get in touch with the folks at Guinness to get more information from them. They will also tell you if your proposal for a new category is acceptable. Good luck. See page 155 for the e-mail address, or write them at:

The Guinness Book of Records, Guinness Media, Inc., 6 Landmark Square, Stamford, CT 06901 U.S.A.

Now, about those food records:

- The biggest watermelon grown weighed in at 117.9 kilograms, in 1990. Bill Carson of Arrington, Tennessee, won that category.
- Gerry Checkon of Spangler, Pennsylvania had the biggest pumpkin grown — a walloping 509 kilograms — in1999.
- The biggest pineapple was the 13-kilogram monster grown in 1978 in Tarauaca, Brazil.
- The largest pizza ever baked was 33.9 metres in diameter. It was made in 1990 by Pizza Hut at the World Trade Center in Singapore.
- The largest hamburger ever made was 2540 kilograms, made in 1989 at the Outagamie County Fairgrounds in Seymour, Wisconsin.
- The world's largest Jell-O was 35 000 litres of watermelon-flavoured pink Jell-O. Paul Squires and Geoff Ross of Brisbane, Australia, made it in 1981.
- Palm Dairies Ltd. in Edmonton, Alberta, made the world's largest ice cream sundae in 1998. It weighed 24 908.8 kilograms and contained: 20 270.7 kilos of ice cream, 4394.4 kilos of syrup and 243.7 kilos of topping.

Why is there fizz in our sodas? What is pop made out of?

More than 2000 years ago, Hippocrates, who has been called the "Father of Medicine," believed that the fizzy mineral waters from natural mineral springs were beneficial to health. So the early Greeks and Romans began to use them for bathing. Later on, during the Middle Ages, people started drinking the waters, and claimed that they were healthy tonics.

English chemist Joseph Priestley is famous for his work with gases and for discovering oxygen. But Priestley also invented soft drinks. He got interested in science after he met inventor Benjamin Franklin, who was visiting London in 1766. Priestley started doing experiments that involved dissolving different gases in water.

The story goes that Priestley lived beside a brewery, and became aware of a gas that was produced by the fermenting grain used to make ale. He figured out how to produce the gas, carbon dioxide, and discovered that it tasted tangy and was fizzy when it was mixed with water. That was the beginning of carbonated water or seltzer water. Five years later, by 1772, Priestley had built a machine to produce carbonated water. The navy used these machines to improve the quality of drinking water aboard ship on long voyages. Priestly then wrote a book about his findings: *Directions for Impregnating Water with Fixed Air, In Order To Communicate To It The Peculiar Spirit And Virtues Of Pyrmont Water, And Other Mineral Waters Of A Similar Nature.* (Whew!)

A few years later Torbern Bergman, a Swedish chemist, figured out how to make large quantities of carbonated water, using chalk to produce the carbonic gas. Simons and Rundell of South

Carolina got the first U.S. patent for mass manufacture of "imitation mineral waters" in 1810, but carbonated drinks didn't become popular until after 1830. At first the drinks were unflavoured and were sold mostly by pharmacists. Eventually fruit syrups and herbs were added. Lemon-flavoured soft drinks came first; ginger ale and root beer became popular later.

One of the big problems was trying to keep the carbon dioxide bubbles from escaping from the beverages. In 1892 a machine shop operator in Baltimore, William Painter, came up with the "Crown Cork Bottle Seal" that kept the beverages from going "flat." By 1920 more than 5000 bottlers existed across the U.S.

Originally the drinks were called seltzers, after a famous German mineral spring. Eventually they were all called "soft drinks," to distinguish them from "hard" or alcoholic drinks. They were recommended as a substitute for liquor. The nickname has always been "soda" because of the bicarbonate of soda that was used to produce carbon dioxide. We also call soda "pop" because the first bottles were stoppered with corks that popped when they were opened.

• The largest ice cream soda float ever made used 337.5 litres of ice cream and 6615 litres of Coca Cola. The concoction was made at North Druid Hill in Atlanta, Georgia, on April 3, 1998.
• Industry statistics say that the average Canadian consumes 116.8 litres of soft drinks a year.
• Total annual sales exceed 3.5 billion litres — equivalent to more than six canned soft drinks a week for every person in Canada.
• Colas are the most popular soft drinks, and account for about three-quarters of all soft drinks sold.

Why do refrigerators turn bananas black? And why do bananas get bruised as they age?

Rolina van G., Mt. Brydges, Ontario

These two questions have related answers. Bananas go black as they age, but those aren't bruises. Even bananas that have never been touched will go black. That's because ethylene, a natural hormone, ripens the fruit . . . but doesn't know when to quit. There's no way of stopping the production of ethylene, although you can slow it down by finding a place that isn't as cold as a refrigerator but is cooler than your kitchen counter. When you put the banana in the refrigerator, it produces another compound called polyphenals, which also turn them black. Cold temperatures, which are foreign to bananas' natural tropical environment, kill the surface cells on the banana peel, and that's what produces the polyphenals.

Check it out though. Black or not, if the banana hasn't over-ripened it will be fine under its covering. You can even freeze bananas. If you coat peeled bananas in chocolate first you have a fabulous frozen treat.

Some authorities say that chimpanzees and other primates go for the whole banana, peel and all. Others say primates *do* peel bananas before eating them and that they peel their bananas from the opposite end that we use. Next time you're at a zoo, see for yourself how they eat their bananas.

59.

When you want to boil water, is it faster to start with hot or cold?

It's faster to start with hot water. If someone took two identical pots, filled one with hot water and the other with the same amount of cold water, then put them on two identical stove burners at identical settings, it would be obvious which would boil first.

Recipe books tend to suggest starting with cold water, but that's so you don't assume they mean for you to use boiling water when that's not what they want. Cold tap water is also likely to be safer for human consumption, because hot water can contain more dissoved minerals.

How about freezing water — what's faster, hot or cold?

Not surprisingly, cold water beats hot water from the tap at the freezing race. But not by more than fifteen minutes (at least for a tray of ice cubes), so it is hardly worth worrying about. However, if two buckets were set outside on a freezing day — one with very hot water at 95°C, and the other at 50°C, the hot water would freeze first!

What gives? Well, there are a number of factors at play. If the water is hot enough, evaporation will take away some of the mass of the water, so there is less to freeze. And hot water will likely "supercool," which means that rather than a thin layer of ice starting on top and freezing down from what becomes an insulated covering, the ice starts to form from within and freezes fast. The other factors include convection, dissolved gases and conduction — but basically, with much hotter water, the hot beats the cold. See the Web site listed on page 155.

How much Kraft Macaroni and Cheese Dinner does the average kid eat?

Lisa E., Edmonton, Alberta

Kraft Dinner, or Kraft Macaroni and Cheese as it is known as in the U. S., is the ultimate comfort food. It's called Kraft Dinner in Canada, where the population eats more "KD" or "Vitamin K" per capita than anywhere else in the world. (This was long before the band, The Barenaked Ladies, made Kraft Dinner so famous in their song ,"If I Had a Million Dollars.")

But before we get onto why kids love this unusual orange delicacy so much, let's just pause to praise pasta for a moment. Spaghetti came to North America mostly in the 1920s with the wave of immigration from southern Italy. The story goes that Prohibition (a period when the production and sale of liquor was illegal in the U. S.) helped the popularity of pasta because you could find a glass of wine at some Italian restaurants, where spaghetti was the main dish sold. People started trying pasta . . . and liking it. Pasta caught on fast. It is cheap, quick and easy for even the least experienced cook to prepare. Boil water. Throw in pasta. Bingo: dinner.

We eat more pasta every year, and it's good for us. It's a complex carbohydrate which gives us six of the eight essential amino acids. There's only a gram of fat in a cup of cooked pasta, and only 210 calories. And word has it that eating pasta releases seratonin, a chemical in the brain that tells you that you're feeling relaxed and calm. That means there is scientific proof that pasta is comfort food. So that means also that those crafty people at Kraft have figured out a way to keep us feeling comfortable.

So what about the little blue box of Kraft Dinner? It is a success story based on smart marketing. Back in the 1930s, during the Depression, Kraft was selling grated cheese in little 2-ounce (56-gram) packages to add to soup or baked dishes. A macaroni salesman for Tenderoni Macaroni in St. Louis tried to figure out how to sell more of the little elbows. He tied one of the Kraft cheese packages onto the macaroni package with a rubber band, and convinced retailers to sell them as a unit. The first blue boxes were 19¢ (this was 1936 when steak was 26¢ a pound) and the slogan was "make a meal for four in nine minutes." Because of the Depression, there was a huge need for inexpensive meatless meals, and Kraft sold 9 million boxes the first year.

Kraft Canada says that if all the boxes of Kraft Dinner sold each year in Canada were lined up end-to-end, they would stretch more than 16 000 kilometres, or from Ottawa to Melbourne, Australia. In fact, the 30 million of us eat 245 000 boxes a day.

What are our favourite foods to enjoy with KD? Kraft's Consumer Response Department says that vegetables, ground beef, tuna and hot dogs are the most popular KD enhancers. The purists add nothing. Why is KD still so popular? Convenience and price are important, but nostalgia plays a big part in the sales of KD too. Lots of people who grew up eating KD keep a box in their cupboard just in case. You never know when you'll need comfort and convenience.

My mom says that putting vinegar in the water you use to boil eggs will keep them from cracking. How does this work?

At the risk of saying that perhaps your mother isn't always right, the truth is that putting vinegar in the water will not stop the eggs from cracking. But it is still a good thing to do.

The wider end of the egg contains an air sac, and this air expands when it gets heated. If it expands really quickly, the pressure will crack the egg's shell. The way to stop this from happening is to make a tiny hole in that end of the egg with a sharp needle, before you cook it. The hole will allow the expanding air to escape, without cracking the shell.

But your mom was on the right track, as there is a reason to put a few drops of vinegar in the water before you cook your eggs. It makes the egg white coagulate so that if the shell *does* crack, less of the white will seep out of the egg when you're cooking it.

• How can you tell if an egg is hard-boiled?
Try spinning it. If it spins freely and uniformly,
then it's cooked. But if the spin is wobbly,
it's raw.
• Did you know that eggs are one of nature's
most perfect foods? The only vitamin they lack
is vitamin C.

63.

Why do hot dog buns come in packages of twelve when hot dogs only come in eight?

Alexandra P., Oromocto, New Brunswick

This seems pretty dopey, and it is just as annoying if you live in the United States, where hot dogs often come in packages of ten and buns in eight or twelve. Not everyone does it this way, but rarely do you find that the numbers match.

What's going on? Basically, it's because the two industries don't think about each other much. The meat packers like things in neatly measured quantities like 500 grams, a kilogram or a pound. (The metric system is used everywhere in the world except the U.S. There are 2.2 pounds to a kilogram, so packages are most often either 454 grams, which is exactly a pound, or 500 grams, which is 1.1 pounds or 0.5 kilograms.) If you look at your package of wieners, the net weight is likely one of these even numbers, and they have packaged the number of wieners that make up that weight. In the U.S. the wieners are generally one-tenth of a pound, so come ten to the package.

Then what about buns? Bakeries tend to sell things by the dozen or in eights, and that's really all there is to it. Of course it also has to do with the size of the pans, and eights or twelves also package up nicely. (Plus, bakers have been going with a system based on "a dozen" for centuries.) So the explanation is as dopey as the problem: two industries that need each other for sales but never seem to think of each other when they figure out the really big questions in life, like how many buns or hot dogs to put in a package.

Why does eating asparagus make urine smell funny?

Rory V., Vancouver, B.C.

Asparagus is really good for you but, *whoo, boy*, that smell can be bizarre. Why? Urine removes waste products from the body and provides valuable information about your urologic and general health. You pass more urine when you drink more liquids and eat more foods that contain more water, such as fruits and vegetables.

The normal smell of urine comes from the acid in it. In diabetics, urine may have a fruity odour due to the presence of excessive glucose. Or if the patient has a urinary tract infection, the urine may have a foul smell. Certain foods may create a characteristic odour as well — things like coffee, asparagus and some vitamins.

But about this particular smell. It is indeed true that eating asparagus can cause some people to produce urine with a temporarily odd smell — sort of a rotten cabbage smell. Back in 1702 a Frenchman, Dr. Louis Lemery, stated in his *Treatise of All Sorts of Foods*, "Sparagrass eaten to Excess sharpen the Humours and heat a little, and therefore persons of a bilious constitution ought to use them moderately. They cause a filthy and disagreeable Smell in the Urine, as every Body knows." The story even goes that at a venerable British men's club there is a sign reading: DURING THE ASPARAGUS SEASON MEMBERS ARE REQUESTED NOT TO RELIEVE THEMSELVES IN THE HATSTAND.

Why that really awful smell? Because two sulphur-containing compounds in asparagus convert during digestion in your body into a closely related compound that has that very distinctive cabbage-ish-sulphur-ish-ammonia-ish rotten odour!

The weird thing is that it doesn't happen to everybody. For years it was assumed that this happened to anyone who ate asparagus, but a study conducted with asparagus eaters indicated that of 800, only 344 produced the odorous substance. The researchers concluded that only about 40% of people have a gene that somehow causes this reaction. In fact, they think that every body excretes methanethiol (the compound that stinks), but that the ability to detect its odour varies from person to person. Apparently this is also an inherited trait. By the way, if you are in that unlucky 40%, you don't have to eat much asparagus. As few as five or six spears is enough to produce a pronounced odour.

So, in fact, there can be four responses to eating those succulent green stalks of asparagus: There are those who can both make it and smell it, those who can make it but not smell it, those who can smell it but not make it themselves, and those who neither make it nor smell it. Who says life is dull?

Some Asparagus Facts:

- It was a delicacy in Greek and Roman times. It was so popular and expensive that many people had to be content with another early spring vegetable, leeks, which were called "poor man's asparagus."
- The ancient Egyptians were so keen on asparagus that they offered it to their gods.

Where did Silly Putty come from?

and Other Intriguing Info About INVENTIONS

65.

Where did Silly Putty come from?

Eirian V., Vancouver, B.C.

It came from the mind of a Scottish engineer in New Haven, Connecticut, during World War II. James Wright was working at General Electric on a contract for the U.S. government, trying to come up with an inexpensive substitute for synthetic rubber. Silly Putty was a fluke — a remarkable outcome of his experimenting, and one that he certainly never expected.

Wright noticed that when he dropped boric acid into silicone oil he got goofy pink goo that stretched and bounced more than rubber. And the bonus was that the stuff could pick up images from comic books or newspapers. It could be molded, too. But . . . what could they do with it? Nothing. It was no good as a synthetic rubber substitute — it was just . . . well . . . nutty. Maybe that's why GE called it "nutty putty."

Things began to change when some scientists started taking it to parties. In 1949 at a cocktail party with a bunch of executives, a toy store owner happened to watch people stretching, bouncing and shaping the stuff. Advertising copywriter Peter Hodgson, a Montrealer by birth, was at that party too. Hodgson and the toy store owner decided it would be smart to put a description in the toy store's catalogue and sell it for two dollars as an adult's toy. It sold fabulously, but the toy store just wasn't interested in marketing it further.

Hodgson, who had been calling it "Gupp" until he came up with "Silly Putty," decided to go for it. He took a risk and bought 9.5 kilograms of the goo for $147.00 (which he had to borrow!). Since Easter was coming, he hired a student to help him chop it up into small portions and put them into coloured plastic eggs, with the slogan, "the toy with one moving part." The mark-up was huge: he sold his 672 eggs for $2.00 each — that's about $1.78 profit per egg (minus labour and the eggshell).

At first, sales were mildly successful — just 300 eggs a day — but what made them take off was a mention in *The New Yorker*'s "Talk of the Town" that August. In four days Hodgson had a quarter of a million orders. He quickly got into mass-manufacturing the stuff, shipping the eggs in egg cartons, and becoming a very wealthy man. Eventually he moved into a mansion that folks called "Silly Putty Estate." And all that success was in marketing just to adults!

Hodgson quickly figured out that there was a huge market for children, but the kids were getting putty stuck onto carpets and their clothes. By 1960 the manufacturers replaced the formula with one that was non-sticky. Today Silly Putty is mostly thought of as a kids' toy. Hand an egg to most adults, though, and they know what to do with it.

Silly Putty can be used for:

- cleaning keys on piano or computer keyboards
- keeping tools from floating around in zero gravity (if you happen to be an astronaut)
- removing lint from clothing
- steadying wobbly tables
- taking casts of footprints
- plugging leaks

Make some Silly Puttyish Goo-like Slime:

Mix 155mL of white glue with 125mL of water in a plastic bottle or glass jar with a lid. Tint with food colouring.

In another plastic bottle or jar, mix 40mL

of laundry borax (20-Mule Team) with 500mL water.

Pour 60mL of the glue mixture into a small paper cup.

While stirring, add 30mL of the borax solution.

You will have instant putty. Take it out of the cup, rinse it and pat it dry with paper towels. You can store it in a self-sealing plastic bag for several days.

How were M&Ms invented?

Chris and Jesse, by e-mail

Like many inventions, you could never guess how this sweet treat came into being. Forrest Mars Senior of Mars Candies was travelling in Spain during the Spanish Civil War. He saw soldiers eating what looked like pellets of candy. They were chocolates in a hard sugary coating. Sound familiar? The coating was there so the chocolate wouldn't melt. Mars thought this was a great idea and went home to invent the recipe for M&Ms plain chocolate candies.

The public first saw these in 1941, but American GIs serving in World War II had tried them before because M&Ms were included in their food rations, packaged in tubes. The military liked this snack, since it travelled well in many climates. By the end of the 1940s M&Ms were popular with the public, and the tube gave way to the familiar brown pouch. In 1954 M&Ms Peanut Chocolate Candies were introduced, and that same year came the M&M characters and the slogan, "the milk chocolate melts in your mouth, not in your hand."

M&M stands for Mars and Murrie, after Forrest Mars and Bruce Murrie, who developed the candy.

67.

Who invented the first video game system?

Rajkumar P., Toronto, Ontario

Credit for the first video game goes to Steve Russell. In 1962 Russell was a computer programmer at the Massachusetts Institute of Technology (MIT), which had received a donation of a computer from Digital Equipment Corporation (DEC). DEC wanted to see what the bright young programmers at MIT could do with the Digital PDP-1 computer. Little did they know that a game called Spacewar would be the result!

There was one big problem though. The computer that ran the game was a mainframe computer that took up the floor space of a small house! It was also very expensive (several million dollars), and only the biggest corporations and universities could afford it. Spacewar was a two-player game that involved spaceships firing photon torpedoes at each other. (Pretty simple stuff compared to what you can now do on a laptop.)

Credit for getting the arcade video game industry going goes to Nolan Bushnell. In 1971 he took over his daughter's bedroom to develop a much simpler machine that could play the Spacewar game. (His daughter had to sleep on the couch.) The computer business is all about timing, and Bushnell's timing was just right. The silicon computer chip had just been developed, making it possible to build smaller and cheaper computers. He called his arcade game Computer Space. Unfortunately it was a total flop, mostly because people didn't know how to play it!

Bushnell realized that he needed to develop a game based on one that people already knew. So Pong (based on ping-pong) was born. Pong was introduced at a bar in Sunnyvale, California, in 1971. The game was such a hit that the machine became too full of quarters and broke down!

Bushnell then started a company called Atari, after the word a samurai uses to warn his opponent that he is about to be attacked. Atari sold 10 000 copies of Pong. Lots of other companies imitated it, and it became the most popular coin-operated game around. In 1975 Sears sold the first home version of Pong, to be played on a television set. People lined up outside stores for hours to get their hands on a game. For many of us, video games were our first introduction to using computers, and have been credited with getting computers into our homes.

Check out the Web site (page 155) for more info.

68.

What the heck does "Pez" mean?

Bill M., Squamish, B.C.

It's a shortened form of the German word for peppermint: *pfefferminz*. Pez has been around since 1927, when it was created in Vienna, Austria. At first these mini-sized, soap-shaped candies came in only one flavour — peppermint — and they were meant for adults. They arrived in the U. S. in 1950 in a plain dispenser. No Garfield heads, snowmen or cellphone replicas. By 1952 the manufacturers added fruit flavours and cartoon heads, beginning with Popeye. Now the folks at Pez (who call their product the pioneer of "interactive candy") have produced hundreds of dispensers over the years, spawning collectors galore. Pez sells over 3 billion candies a year in the U. S. alone — no peppermint flavour anymore, though — as well as in 60 countries around the world.

69.

When Ben Franklin invented electricity and he got electrocuted, why didn't he die?

Brittany D., by e-mail

Benjamin Franklin was born in 1706, the fifteenth child of seventeen, and the youngest son. He went to school in Boston for only two years because his family could not afford to pay for his education. He taught himself algebra, geometry, navigation, logic and science. He also learned French, German, Italian, Spanish and Latin, and became one of the best-educated men of his time.

Franklin was one of the first people to experiment with electricity, but he was very lucky that he was not killed while flying his famous kite. Franklin suspected that lightning was a form of electricity, so on June 10, 1752, he decided to test his idea. There are lots of misconceptions about this experiment because Franklin never wrote about it. He did tell his colleague, Joseph Priestly, and Priestly wrote it down — but not until 15 years after it happened.

Franklin made a kite from a large silk handkerchief and two cross-sticks, with a wire pointer fixed to it. He attached a metal key to the bottom of the kite's string. The string was made of hemp (a weak conductor) on the upper portion, and silk ribbon (a non-conductor) on the lower.

With the help of his son he launched the kite during an approaching thunderstorm. After a while he noticed that some of the threads on the hemp part of the string were sticking straight out, so he touched his knuckle to the key and observed an electric spark. The kite and hemp string had collected the electric current in the air and then charged the metal key. This confirmed Franklin's idea that lightning is actually a large electric spark.

Franklin wasn't stupid. He had suspected that lightning was a very powerful electric force. That's why he launched the kite just as the thunderstorm was approaching. Had a lightning bolt actually hit his kite he probably would have died instantly. So Franklin wasn't really electrocuted while doing his kite experiment.

Franklin used his knowledge of lightning to invent the lightning rod. It's a metal rod that is attached to the roof of a building. A wire made out of copper or aluminum runs from the rod into a conductive grid buried in the ground. If the rod is struck by lightning, the system carries the electrical current down the rod, through the wire and into the ground — without causing damage to the building.

Franklin's experiments did involve risk, though. One time he tried to kill a turkey with an electric shock, but instead *he* got shocked. He said, "I meant to kill a turkey, and instead, I almost killed a goose."

- When you see a flash of lightning, start counting the seconds until you hear thunder, and then divide the number of seconds by 3. That will tell you, in kilometres, how close the lightning is to you. (Sound travels about 1 kilometre in 3 seconds.)
- Lightning kills about 12 people in Canada each year, and 10 times that many in the U.S.
- Franklin was the only man who signed all four of the following key documents in American history: the Declaration of Independence, the Treaty of Alliance with France, the Treaty of Peace with Great Britain and France, and the Constitution of the United States.

Why and where was the pretzel invented?

Aaron V., Carson, California

Think about the shape of the pretzel. Think Middle Ages. Think monks. Thought of anything yet?

The story goes that an Italian monk invented the pretzel during the Middle Ages. He rolled long strips of bread dough and shaped it to resemble arms crossed in prayer. After baking, he gave them out as treats to children who had memorized their prayers.

It's also possible that the word comes from the Latin *pretzola*, which means "little reward."

You can make your own big soft pretzels and treat your friends, whether they memorize something or not.

Make Your Own Pretzels:

250mL water
1 8-gram package active dry yeast
30 mL sugar
5 mL salt
750mL all-purpose flour, unsifted
15 mL butter at room temperature
1 beaten egg yolk
coarse salt

Mix 230mL of the flour with the sugar, salt
  and undissolved yeast.
Heat 230mL water and butter for 35 seconds
  in a microwave.
Gradually add to dry ingredients, beat
  2 minutes at medium speed of mixer.
Add 100mL flour.
Beat at high speed 2 minutes.

Stir in enough additional flour to make a soft dough.

On floured board, knead 5 minutes.

Set in greased bowl; turn to grease top of dough.

Cover and let rise in warm, draft-free place for 40 minutes.

Preheat oven to 190°C.

Divide dough into 12 equal pieces.

Roll each into a 50-cm rope.

Shape into pretzels or other shapes.

Place on greased baking sheets.

Cover; let rest 5 minutes.

Mix egg yolk and 20mL water; brush on pretzels.

Sprinkle with coarse salt.

Bake 15 minutes, or until done.

Cool on racks.

Why do bulls like red?

and Other ODDS AND ENDS

Why do bulls like red?

Christine H. and Jeff G., by e-mail

They don't, but they certainly fooled you. It isn't the red at all. Bulls charge because the matador is swinging the cape around, and bulls have been trained to charge the cape. It's the motion that gets them going, not the colour.

But let's go back a bit. What's with bullfighting anyway? The first fight was in Spain in 1133, honouring the coronation of King Alfonso VIII. For about 500 years this wild spectacle was reserved for commemorating big events or entertaining important guests. Then it became more widespread and popular with the common folk.

Slaying bulls has always been a controversial practice. In the mid-1500s Pope Pius V tried to stop bullfighting, but he was ignored. It is still hugely popular in Spain and the Latin American countries of Mexico, Guatemala, Panama, Peru, Colombia, Ecuador and Venezuela. France and Portugal also have it, but the Portuguese fight from horseback, and the bull isn't killed.

One thing is clear. You can't fight a bull — it's going to win. What the matadors are trying to do is avoid the beast by using their wits, grace and dexterity. Which brings us back to the red cape. In fact, matadors often start with a larger magenta (pinkish-purple) and yellow cape called a *capote*, and then go to a smaller red cape, the *muleta*. The cape is a moving target, which helps keep the bull (who has poor eyesight to start with) focussed. Of course, he is focussed on the cape that keeps moving, so the matador can manipulate the bull all over the place — specifically, away from his own body.

Why red? For the benefit of the fans. It stands out in contrast to the plainer colours of the ring, making it easy for the spectators to see the bullfighter. And the colour red excites people, so they enjoy the bullfight more if the matador swings a red cape.

72. Why are barns red?

Because other barns are red. That's a dopey answer, but it is partially true. The truth is that the first barns weren't painted at all. Most farmers couldn't afford paint, and besides, they thought it was showy and just not done. But in the late nineteenth century, farmers started painting their barns a dark red. No one knows exactly why, but likely the best theory is that red oxide is quite inexpensive, and could be mixed with milk or linseed oil to make red paint. The red oxide pigments came from Binney & Smith (the Crayola people), who have always been in the colour business. Of course, paint helps preserve wood — that would appeal to the thrifty farmers. And the red looks so good with the green fields. Once red was established as the barn colour, paint manufacturers took off with it.

Not all barns are red actually. Sometimes they are white, green, blue or grey. The colour tends to depend on the area, as folks do what their neighbours do, or what their ethnic tradition suggests. In some parts of central Kentucky, barns and fences and other farm buildings are black. That came from using lampblack and diesel fuel. (It's a really cheap wood preservative, but imagine the smell — and don't light a match!)

73.

Why do most TV and radio stations start their names with a W or K?

Matt, Kentucky

In the U.S., "call letters" usually begin with W or K. In Canada they usually start with C. Why? There is an international treaty monitored by the International Telecommunications Union in Geneva, Switzerland, that specifies the first call letters for commercial broadcast stations in different countries: Mexico is X, for example, and Canada is C. This is how operators keep radio, TV, ship-to-shore and aircraft telecommunications straight. The U.S. uses K and W, although since they are so large geographically and have so many radio stations, they actually use A and N too. You would likely only run into call letters starting with N and A if you were involved with the navy and coast guard or amateur radio.

In 1934 the U.S. Communications Act stated that broadcasters west of the Mississippi River use K call signs, and W for east of the Mississippi. There are a few exceptions to this rule, as some radio stations were in business before 1934, like KYW in Philadelphia, KDKA and KDQ in Pittsburgh, and WHO in Des Moines.

Before 1912, radio stations could use any call sign they wanted. A few of the surviving three-letter call signals were from the days before the call-sign legislation, when stations came up with their own names. In Chicago WGN was first owned by the Chicago Tribune Newspaper and stands for "World's Greatest Newspaper." WLS for "World's Largest Store," was owned by Sears Roebuck.

Armed with this knowledge, you can usually figure out airplane and boat registration too, since they use the same first letters as the broadcasters.

74.

Why does the water in the toilet flush the opposite way in Australia? What would happen if you flushed it right on the equator?

David R., Thunder Bay, Ontario

Time out. Toilets, sinks and bathtubs don't necessarily drain the opposite way south of the equator. It's a widespread myth that they do, because of the earth's rotation. (An episode of "The Simpsons" was even devoted to the topic.) But it is a myth. Check out sinks and toilets and bathtubs around you. They all drain slightly differently, because of several reasons — the way they were manufactured, how the water squirts into the bowl, and the way the drain is shaped — *not* because of the rotation of the earth. This is true in both hemispheres and on the equator.

Okay, why would we think they drain differently, in the first place? Because of what is called the Coriolis Force. The rotation direction of hurricanes, for example, depends on the Coriolis Force, among other natural forces. These forces make very large things like cyclones, hurricanes, tornadoes and even ocean currents spin counterclockwise in the Northern Hemisphere and clockwise in the Southern Hemisphere. The Coriolis Force doesn't affect the drainage in your tub, sink or toilet, though, because the drainage action lasts such a short time. See the Web site (page 155) for more on this.

The word "john" for toilet may date back as far as fifteenth-century England. Instead of outhouse they called it Jack's house or Jake's house. It could also be called Cousin John's, then just john.

75.

How does the non-stick surface stick to the pan?

When you paint a smooth surface you have to rough it up a bit with sandpaper to get the paint to stick. It's a similar principle with pans. The first non-stick pans were made either by blasting the pan with grit to make little pits in the aluminum, or by spraying it with some kind of a lumpy coating. This gave the non-stick stuff something to cling to.

But it was still hard to get the non-stick stuff to stick, and it was very easy to damage the pan's surface with a fork or other metal tool. Also, after a while the non-stick stuff would start to peel off. So the manufacturers tried adding a sticky molecule to the non-sticky molecule and applying this to the pitted pan first, as a primer. Then a coat of non-sticky stuff was put over that, and finally another layer of non-stick with some kind of "toughener" was put on the top to protect the non-stick layer. Lots of non-stick pans are still made this way.

Teflon was DuPont's original brand name for the non-stick coating. Roy J. Plunkett, a chemist, discovered this tetrafluoroethylene resin accidentally in 1938. It was very heat-tolerant, and so slippcry that virtually nothing would stick *to* it or be absorbed *by* it. DuPont registered the name Teflon in 1945. Today there are Plunkett Awards given for "innovation with Teflon."

These days DuPont has come up with a new way — called "smooth technology" — to get the Teflon to stick to the pan. The pan is not pitted first. Instead, a new kind of sticky molecule is used that can "lock" itself to the smooth pan. This lets the next layers fuse together better, so that the pan is more durable. However, metal tools and high heat (which softens the non-stick molecules) are still the enemies of non-stick pans.

• Teflon is one of the few substances the human body doesn't reject, so it is used in making heart pacemakers, artificial eyes, substitute bones and replacement hip and knee joints. It has also been used in outer space on electrical wires, nose cones, fuel tanks, and the outer skins of spacesuits to shield them against the heat of the sun.

• Some authorities claim that parakeets and other small birds can be harmed by exposure to fumes from heated non-stick pans, so don't hang your budgie cage near the stove — for more than one reason.

76. What is that swirly thing at the barber's shop, the one with red and blue and white stripes that twirl?

Kristine U., Sierra Madre, California

The short answer is that it's called a barber pole, but how it came to be is the interesting part. When you go to get your hair cut, how would you feel about having a tooth pulled out at the same time? For six centuries in Europe, that is exactly what could happen, because barbers could practise surgery too. They were called barber surgeons, and by 1361 they had their own religious guild (like a professional association), which became a trade guild by 1462. The barbers' and surgeons' guilds didn't separate until 1745. Barber surgeons did a lot of bloodletting in those days.

And what exactly is bloodletting? It used to be prescribed for lots of diseases, even for fevers or hemorrhaging (internal bleeding). Be glad you live in these times. Barbers got into the bloodletting business in 1163 when the Pope decided that the monks had to stop doing it.

And here's where the barber pole comes in. It symbolizes that bloodletting business. The patients would get a strong grip on a staff or pole, to make their veins stick out, then (among other methods) the barber would attach leeches to the person, and catch the blood in a basin. Then they'd bandage up the patient with strips of linen.

Believe it or not, those bloody bandages would often be hung outside on the staff to advertise the barber surgeon's practice. They would twirl in the wind, inspiring the spiral pattern of red and white that was eventually painted on poles to advertise the barber business. The first poles even had a leech basin on top, which eventually became the ball. Nowadays blue is added to red and white on the poles, perhaps representing the blue veins along with the red blood and white bandages. (You may never feel quite the same about getting your hair cut at a barbershop again!)

What did the judge say to the dentist?
Do you swear to pull the tooth, the whole tooth and nothing but the tooth?

77.

What is the highest number?

Hunter R., London, England

The very biggest number that actually has a name is googolplex. One googol is 1 followed by 100 zeros, or 10 to the 100th power or 10^{100}. If you write it out it looks like this:

10,000,000,000,000,000,000,000,000,
000,000,000,000,000,000,000,000,000,000,
000,000,000,000,000,000,000,000,000,000,
000,000,000,000,000.

Edward Kasner, an American mathematician, popularized the term googol in 1938. His eight-year-old nephew came up with the name googol when his uncle asked him to make up what he thought a huge number would be called.

Kasner came up with googolplex too. It is 10 to the googol in power, or 10 followed by a googol zeros: $10^{10^{100}}$. Printing that out would take up the rest of this book, so we won't.

But that's the largest *named* number. The truth is, there is no largest number, because whatever number you can get up to (say a septillion) you can always add 1 . . . then 1 more . . . then 1 more . . .

Useful Facts:

The number 1,000,000,000,000,000 is called different names in different countries. Here's how it works in North America.

1,000 is one thousand.
1,000,000 is one million.
1,000,000,000 is one billion.
1,000,000,000,000 is one trillion.
1,000,000,000,000,000 is one quadrillion.
1,000,000,000,000,000,000 is one quintillion.

In Great Britain the first two are the same, but:

1,000,000,000 is one thousand million, or one milliard.

1,000,000,000,000 is one billion.

1,000,000,000,000,000 is one thousand billion.

1,000,000,000,000,000,000 is one trillion.

Of course, this can get confusing, since once you get past a million, the numbers are different. The British media and government tend to use the North American meaning, although within the British legal system, they may use the British terminology.

There's no such thing as a "zillion." It's just slang for a really big number. Now you can use more precise names! A great place to learn more on this topic is Ask Dr. Math. See p. 155 for the Web site.

Name That Number:

- quadrillion:
  1,000,000,000,000,000
- quintillion:
  1,000,000,000,000,000,000
- sextillion:
  1,000,000,000,000,000,000,000
- septillion:
  1,000,000,000,000,000,000,000,000
- octillion:
  1,000,000,000,000,000,000,000,000,000
- nontillion:
  1,000,000,000,000,000,000,000,000,000,000
- decillion:
  1,000,000,000,000,000,000,000,000,000,000,000

Why is it called WD-40?

WD-40 is slippery stuff that solves a lot of problems — spray a little on your bike chain, or on a squeaky door hinge. It was called that because the folks at Rocket Chemical, a small company of only three employees that developed WD-40, got it right on the 40th try. WD stands for water displacement.

Is it true only boys can be colour-blind?

and Other Surprises About THE OPPOSITE SEX

79.

Is it true only boys can be colour-blind?

Diane K., Toronto, Ontario

No, but while 8% of boys can't distinguish various colours and shades, less than half of 1% of girls are colour-blind. The professionals call it colour vision deficiency, which describes the problem better — difficulty determining various colours and shades.

We all have cones and rods at the back of our eyes that help us detect the differences in colours and degrees of brightness. If you are colour-blind there are varying degrees of problems with those cones, or just fewer cones. Mostly you are born with this, but some older adults develop troubles distinguishing one dark colour from another as they age, or if they develop a retinal disease.

The most common problem is red-green colour vision deficiency, which means there aren't enough red and green cones. So in lower lights, folks with this problem might think those colours are brown, or that the green object is red.

Likely you will figure out if you are colour-blind during your school years. And if one of your family members is colour-blind, you have a greater chance of being colour-blind too. It's not considered a disability — more a social inconvenience. If you are affected you may need help coding your clothing to make sure it doesn't clash badly. And figuring out traffic lights will take some training too. So many guys have this problem that it makes you really wonder why red and green are used for warning signals. And remember: be sensitive to your colour-blind friends — they absolutely won't be able to play laser tag with you.

80.

Is it true that the life span of a woman is longer than a man's? Are there more males or females in the world? Why?

Kendra N., by e-mail

Indeed it is true. In most developed countries of the world, women outlive men by 5 to 9 years. In 1995 the life expectancy for females in over 15 nations was at or exceeded 80 years. In Canada life expectancy for females is 81.4 years and for men, 75.8 years. That beats the U.S., where life expectancy for females is 79.4 years and for men is 73.6 years. The World Health Organization reported in 1998 that there were 5.8 billion people in the world, and the global life span was 65 years.

Records for things like life spans started to be kept in the 1500s, so we know that at least since then women have lived longer than men. Cavemen probably only lived to be about 18. Over the past hundred years life expectancy in developed countries has increased 71% for women and 66% for men — mostly due to better nutrition and better health care. Throughout the world, there are nine times more women than men who are over 100 years old. The death rates for women are lower than those for men at all ages, even before birth.

Some scientists believe that females are genetically programmed to live longer so that they can raise their children and maybe even their grandchildren. Sex hormones probably have a lot to do with life span — males have a hormone called testosterone that experts believe is linked to aggressive behaviour and that puts men at higher risk for heart disease. Females have estrogen, which doctors believe protects them from heart disease and strokes until later in life.

You might assume, then, that the world would have more women in it. But it isn't true — according to the United Nations' statistics for the year 2000, there are 3 049 241 000 males and 3 005 808 000 females worldwide. The sex ratio is 101.4 males per 100 females. If girls live longer than boys, how can this be?

It all comes down to the fact that more males are conceived and born than females. At birth, there are about 106 male babies for every 100 female babies. And although more males than females die in every subsequent year of life, it doesn't quite balance out. Between the ages of 15 and 24, males are three times more likely to die than females — and the most common cause of death is from motor vehicle accidents, followed by homicide, suicide, cancer and drowning. Even between the ages of 55 to 64, men in the U.S. are twice as likely as women to die in car accidents. So boys — be careful!

Some scientists believe that life expectancy will continue to rise. Some even think that there is no maximum age, because of medical advances, and that in the future, people will die only because of accidents, not from "old age."

81.

How come tortoise-shell cats are always girls?

Sam H., Peterborough, Ontario

Tortoise-shell and calico cats have a combination of orange/red colouring from one parent, and black, tabby or other non-orange colouring from the other parent. Red, black and cream tortoise-shell cats are almost all female. Same thing with calico cats that are more than half white, with patches of red and black. Funny, isn't it? Only 5 in 1000 are male, and those males are sterile — they can't reproduce. Why?

It all comes down to the way chromosomes work. Females have two X chromosomes (XX) and males have an X and a Y (XY). Turns out that the gene that controls orange/red is an X chromosome, as is the gene for non-red. Since females have the XX pattern, only they can have the two colours. The rare male tortoise-shell cat is a result of an extra X chromosome (an XXY combination) where the male gets all the female colour characteristics with the two XX chromosomes, plus the Y for the male charactcristics.

Because of the rarity of the male tortoisc-shell cat, for many centuries it has been considered good luck to own one. In England it was even believed that you could get rid of warts by having the male tortoise-shell cat's tail rubbed on your warts in the month of May. Japanese fishermen, who would use them to protect their ships from storms and the crews from ghosts, also keenly sought out these cats.

82.

What is a courting candle?

Sandy B., Buttonville, Ontario

Courting is an old fashioned term for seeking affection — dating, wooing or romancing. And a courting candle is a relic of the times before electricity, when parents were very strict with their daughters' affections. The courting candle comes from the nineteenth century, and looks a bit like a candle stuck into a heavy bedspring. The deal was that the suitor could stay until the candle burned down to the level of the top of the holder. Since different kinds of candles burn at different rates, and since the girls' parents could also choose how much of the candle to let stick above the holder, there was room to manipulate the courting situation. A young man would know his girlfriend's parents thought he was okay if the candle was high above the holder and took a very long time to burn down. He got a nice long visit!

Why does hair fall out and why does it only happen to men?

MatrixEfex, by e-mail

Male or female, you lose up to 125 hairs a day. New hairs will replace the lost ones — unless you're balding. And it doesn't just happen to men. Both men and women lose hair density as they grow older, but far more men than women go completely bald.

Why do you go bald? Your hair follicles start shrinking. When those hair follicles can't produce new hair to replace the hair that falls out every day, you have a net loss. Your hair follicles shrink because of hormonal changes, and men have a typical type of balding (called "male pattern baldness") caused by the male hormone testosterone. Researchers also know that your age, your sex, and whether or not your parents were baldies play a part. Basically, don't get too attached to those locks, guys.

Where did the "high-5" come from?

and Other High-Scoring Facts About SPORTS

Where did the "high-5" come from?

Matt S., North Vancouver, B.C.

It seems so common now, but we've only been "high-fiving" since the 1970s. One story goes that Glenn Burke, a major league baseball player with the nickname of King Kong, invented the motion. It was September of 1977, and his team, the Los Angeles Dodgers, was down to its last game of the regular season. Dusty Baker, Burke's teammate, hit a home run and Burke ran to meet him at home plate. He congratulated Baker by leaping into the air and giving him the "high-5." A few minutes later Baker celebrated Burke's first major league home run with a "high-5," of course.

The other story that *Sports Illustrated for Kids* tells is that the "high-5" originated when female volleyball players were jumping to hit the ball during practices. They would often slap one another's hands by accident. Then they started doing it on purpose, to congratulate another player for a good move, or to build team spirit.

Can you hit a baseball farther with an aluminum bat than with a wooden bat?

Denton T., Calgary, Alberta

Yes you can, at least in theory. Why? There are a few good reasons. Aluminum bats are lighter than wooden bats of the same size, so the batter can swing them faster. The weight is more evenly distributed, and the "sweet spot" is larger since the faster swing brings the centre of gravity closer to the batter's body.

What's a "sweet spot"? Find it on your bat and you'll know why it's so sweet. Hold the bat loosely just below the knob on its handle, and let it hang down from your fingers. Ask a friend to gently tap the bat with a hammer, starting at the bottom and working up. Every time the hammer taps the bat you should feel a vibration in your fingers — except when the tap is on the sweet spot. It might also make a slightly different sound. (This spot is also called the bat's centre of percussion.)

When a bat hits a ball, vibrations travel in waves up and down the length of the bat. If the ball hits the bat's sweet spot, the waves cancel each other out. You won't feel any vibrations in your hands, and since very little of the bat's energy is lost to vibrations, more energy can be transferred to the ball. Having a larger sweet spot means that even less energy is lost to vibrations. A high-quality wooden bat has a sweet spot roughly 7.6 centimetres in length. But an aluminum bat the same length has a sweet spot up to three times as large.

Because aluminum is a harder material than wood, an aluminum bat doesn't have as much "give" as a wooden one. So when the ball hits the aluminum bat, little of its kinetic energy is absorbed by the bat — and that energy is retained by the ball. A wooden bat will absorb more of a ball's kinetic energy.

A ball can go as much as 6.4 kilometres per hour faster off an aluminum bat, and the potential distance it can fly is up to 10% farther than if it was hit with a wooden bat. When aluminum bats were first used by the NCAA (The National Collegiate Athletic Association) in the early 1970s, batting averages rose thirty points and the number of home runs that were hit doubled.

Who invented the skateboard, and is it true that skateboarders invented snowboarding and surfing?

Matthew G., by e-mail

Nope, skateboarders didn't invent sidewalk surfing and snowboarding — surfers started it all. They nailed roller skate bases onto wooden planks so that they could sidewalk surf when the weather or waves kept them out of the water. This was back in the 1930s and 1940s. In 1958 when Bill Richards, a surf shop owner, and his son Mark started producing skateboards with wheels from the Chicago Roller Skate Company, sidewalk surfing took off. In 1963 about 100 kids competed in the first skateboard competition at the Pier Avenue Junior School in Hermosa, California. A hit song by Jan and Dean, called "Sidewalk Surfin'," followed in 1964 — a clear sign of how popular skateboarding was becoming.

All this excitement led to the first National Skateboard Championships in 1965. The fad quickly died out, though, partly because there was a lot of concern about reckless riding, which caused cities to start banning skateboards.

But it wasn't gone for long. In 1971 Richard Stevenson patented a newer version of a skateboard design, and in 1973 Frank Nasworthy invented polyurethane wheels that were perfect for surfing on cement. (Up until then the wheels had been made of metal or clay, which didn't grip the road very well.) Another skateboarding craze was underway!

By the late 1970s more than 40 million skateboards had been sold in the U.S. Even Fred Astaire had one — and a broken wrist from falling off his board at the age of 77.

In the late 1970s, a man from Florida, Allan "Ollie" Gelfand, invented the "ollie" and started off a whole new craze of jumping over fixed objects like curbs, benches and walls, and using empty swimming pools and construction sites to skateboard in. Of course there were lots of injuries, and this got people even more worried than the first time around. They started banning skateboards in public parks and on streets and sidewalks. By the 1980s it was hard to find a place where you could use a skateboard.

But skateboarding's been back in a big way since the mid-1990s. And with it has come a whole skater culture: fashions, music, magazines and videos, and skateboard-only parks. According to some people, there are more than 6 million skateboarders in the U.S. alone. It has become the sixth largest participation sport in America.

Skateboarders, also called "riders" or "skaters," practise three skateboarding styles. Freestyle is where skaters do their tricks on level ground and rails, sometimes to music. In Streetstyle, skaters use the features of the urban landscape (curbs, stairs, benches and so on) to do their tricks. Vertical (also called ramp or half-pipe) is considered "extreme" skateboarding.

Some cool skateboarding terms:
• Goofy: You skate goofy if you skate with your right foot forward.
• Sketchy: When you just about — but don't quite — land a trick, you're sketchy.
• Slam: Basically, when you fall off your board and hurt yourself.

Why is breaking a mirror bad luck?

and Other Spooky SUPERSTITIONS

87.

Why is breaking a mirror bad luck?

Haley, Michigan

Seven years of bad luck is only the beginning. A lot of people believe that if you break a mirror there will be a death in the family that year.

So what's the deal with mirrors? We take them for granted now, but it wasn't until the fourteenth century that you could even get a reflective glass mirror like we know today, and then only in Venice, Italy (a major glass-making area). Before that, people used polished metal, and before *that*, any reflective surface was regarded with awe. When people saw themselves reflected in a lake, they thought that reflection was their soul.

Vanity has been regarded as a character flaw through out the ages. Parents tried to tell their children that the devil would get them if they spent too much time admiring themselves. In an ancient Greek myth, a youth named Narcissus fell in love with his own image, and instead of hunting he just admired himself . . . until he starved to death. (That's why a seriously vain person is sometimes be described as having a Narcissus complex.)

The Romans also came up with the notion of seven years of bad luck or bad health if you broke a mirror. Why seven? That was the time the Romans thought it took for life to renew itself. Since a mirror contains your image, or your "life," they applied the seven-year rule to the mirror. Go figure.

It was also believed that in the year a mirror was broken, you would see something tragic take place. That's probably where the death-in-the-family idea comes from. And then there's the fact that mirrors were incredibly expensive, owned only by the wealthy, so if a servant broke one it might take seven years of salary to replace it!

What other superstitions exist about mirrors and luck? Check these out:

- The number of pieces into which a mirror is broken will show how many unlucky years you will have.
- To break a mirror means that you will lose your best friend.

And here's some counter-magic:

- After you have broken seven mirrors you will have good luck.
- Visiting a graveyard at midnight on a starless night can ward off bad luck resulting from a broken mirror.
- If you break a looking glass, bury all the pieces to prevent bad luck.
- To avert the bad luck that comes from breaking a mirror, throw the pieces of glass into a river and all your trouble will be washed downstream.

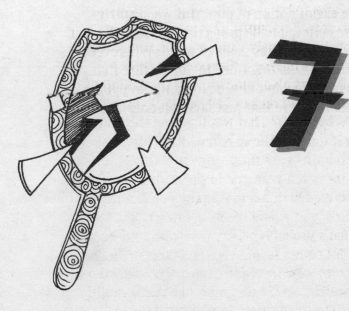

88.

Why do we knock on wood for good luck?

"Touch wood" or "knock on wood" are such common expressions that a lot of people forget that they are superstitions at all. Knocking on wood or touching wood is done to ward off evil, or simply to make sure that what you hope for will happen. It works when you say something like this: "My flu is getting better, knock on wood," and you knock on wood or touch something wooden while you say it.

Why? It ties in to our superstitious fear of boasting or getting too cocky about something, thereby "offending the gods" and making them want to do something to make you know your place — which is lower than theirs. (Greek and Roman mythology is full of stories about the gods cutting humans down to size.) We "knock on wood" so we don't tempt fate to do the opposite of what we want.

Why wood, though? It may be that this came from the pagan notion of powerful wood spirits that were believed to be protective, or from the fact that Christ's cross was made of wood. Wherever it came from, it is so ingrained in our culture that people now often don't even physically touch the wood. They believe that just saying it does the trick.

Why is a rabbit's foot considered lucky?

Since before 600 B.C., folks have thought the whole rabbit to be pretty special — it is both mysterious and lucky. But after St. Augustine converted the Britons to Christianity, pagan (pre-Christian) symbols were banned. Some people still believed in them, but did so in secret.

So instead of worshipping the hare, many Britons carried a hare's *foot*, which they would hide in a pocket. Later, rabbits were introduced from Europe, and the rabbit's foot — more easy to get — took over from the hare's foot. And why the foot, specifically? It is a symbol of potency and speed, and the bone of the hare's foot was said to cure gout and rheumatism.

But why is the rabbit considered lucky? The ancient peoples in Europe thought rabbits had a direct line to nature spirits who happened to live alongside them. Since rabbits produce so many babies so often, people thought the spirits were using the rabbit as a symbol of prosperity and good health. Add it all up, and the rabbit or hare was much revered in pre-Christian times.

To really work as a charm or talisman, people thought that the rabbit's foot had to come from the left hind foot of a rabbit killed at the full moon by a cross-eyed person. To find out more, check out the Easter bunny info on page 82.

90.

Why does touching a toad give you warts, and what cures them?

This is a weird one, as toads are rather clean little fellows. Toads are actually considered lucky because the presence of a toad means there is water around — so no droughts, which generally means that good fortune is ahead. Warts, those annoying but not dangerous skin growths, are in fact from a virus, not from a toad. But since toads have bumpy and wart-like skin, and since the most common location for warts is on the hands, over the years toads have been given a bad rap as the source of warts. Not so. There is even a superstition about getting rid of warts by touching a toad. Also not so.

If you have a wart, talk to your doctor. He or she will likely tell you to use an over-the-counter ointment, to wear the wart down with a pumice stone, or get it surgically cut out or zapped with a laser to kill the roots. It will depend on the wart. There is no "best" treatment, and sometimes warts just go away.

Of course, there are all sorts of folk treatments too, and you never know . . . it might just work to:
- Never think of it or look at it.
- Show it to someone else and don't look at it for nine nights.
- Rub it gently and repeat:
  Anna, mana, meno, mike,
  Paro, Iono, bono, strike,
  Mare, war-e, wallow-wack.
- Put some tears, produced from cutting an onion, on the wart.
- Rub it with a penny and throw the penny away where no one will ever find it.
- Steal a dish rag, go to the woods, turn around three times and throw the rag behind you from your right hand. Go

home and don't go back to that place
for three weeks.

- Wash the wart in dew before breakfast, just
as the sun rises, on the first three mornings
of May.
- Rub a snail on the wart.
- Put a piece of horse manure on a stump.
When the manure is gone, the wart will be
gone.
- Tie a string around the wart, remove the
string and then hang it on the wall. When
the string rots the wart will leave.

Why did people start imagining aliens on Mars?

and Other Offbeat Answers About
STRANGE STUFF

91.

Why did people start imagining aliens on Mars, not some other planet?

Isis M., by e-mail

Maybe it's the reddish glow Mars gives off that has made it an object of fascination since ancient times. Red stood out in the night sky, and the planet didn't move along the same arc as most of the other planets and stars. In fact, the ancient Egyptians called it "the backward traveller" because after moving in one direction for months, it would appear to reverse direction and travel backwards across the sky. The Greeks and Romans were also fascinated by Mars, and came to associate it with war, probably because it is red — the colour of blood and the colour associated with rage. (The Romans' name for their god of war was Mars.) The truth is, Mars is red from rust — it's covered with oxidized minerals that are rich in iron.

The first science fiction writing about space journeys and life on other worlds is from the seventeenth century. By the end of the nineteenth century Mars was a favoured "destination" in science fiction. In the 1800s there was a lot of fascination with the "red planet." Italian astronomer Giovanni Schiaparelli drew maps of the *canali* (the Italian word for "channels") he observed on Mars. English-speaking people thought he meant "canals," and soon people came to believe that there were artificially constructed waterways on Mars . . . and that had to mean there was life on the planet. What Schiaparelli had actually meant was that there were grooves in the surface!

Astronomer Percival Lowell built a private observatory in Flagstaff, Arizona, and started making observations of Mars in 1894. He was convinced that the *canali* were real, and eventually mapped hundreds of them. He believed they were created by a race of intelligent Martians, to carry water from the polar caps to the equatorial regions.

Influenced by Lowell's ideas, in 1898 H. G. Wells published the famous *The War of the Worlds*, in which the Martians — who have been spying on Earth for years — finally invade it.

Astronomers knew that on August 23, 1924, the proximity of Mars and the Earth would be the closest since the beginning of the 1800s, and many people believed this would be the time that Martians would try to contact Earth. Military stations monitored the airwaves for unusual radio signals, but nothing happened.

One of the best remembered Mars "experiences" came on Hallowe'en night, in 1938. Orson Welles, who had a contract with CBS to provide a weekly radio broadcast of adaptations of well-known classics, broadcast *The War of the Worlds* on a radio program. Because it sounded like a news broadcast, many people believed that the Martians actually *were* invading Earth, and there was mass panic. Cars jammed the highways, trying to escape the cities. People had heart attacks. The National Guard was called out. It took days for the Red Cross to convince people that it was safe to return home.

There were movies made about Martians, too: *Flash Gordon: Mars Attacks the World* in 1938, *Abbott and Costello Go to Mars* in 1953, *Robinson Crusoe on Mars* in 1964 and *Mars Attacks!* in 1996.

It turns out that it is possible there was life on Mars, and that Martian life forms have been landing on our planet for billions of years. Scientists have found what they believe is fossil evidence of life that existed on Mars, in meteorites found in Antarctica. The catch, though, is that the fossils are the remains of teeny tiny bacteria — nowhere near the invading aliens we've imagined all these years. See page 155 for a great Web site.

92.

Where and what is the Holy Grail?

Ken H., Nanaimo, B.C.

There's a good chance you know something about Arthurian legends. You might have read *King Arthur and His Knights of the Round Table* or maybe you've seen the movie *Camelot* (1967) or *The Sword in the Stone* (1963). There are thousands of stories based on the legend of King Arthur, the hero of many of these medieval romances. Whether he ever existed, though, is questionable. It is also unknown how, where and when the stories started, though Wales is commonly assumed to be the original setting, perhaps in the sixth century. The whole phenomenon is a fascinating web of history and fable.

It started with one basic tale. Uther Pendragon was king, and when he died all of the knights wanted to claim his crown. Merlin the Magician proposed the idea that the person who could pull the silver sword, Excalibur, out of the stone must be the true king of England. None of the knights could do it, but Arthur could, so he was obviously Pendragon's successor.

A lot of Arthurian literature is hardly about Arthur at all, though. During the Middle Ages the legend began to be about other characters from King Arthur's court: Sir Lancelot and Queen Guinevere, Tristan and Isolde, Galahad, Gawain, Perceval and the Holy Grail.

A grail, probably from the old French word *graal*, is a fairly plain dish or platter — but in medieval literature it became a holy vessel made of gold and inlaid with precious stones. In that story young Perceval, a rather naïve, bumpkin-like knight in Arthur's fellowship, visited the castle of the wounded Fisher King, keeper of the grail. There he saw the beautiful grail in a mystical procession, but because he had been warned not to talk too much, he didn't ask about it. It turned out that if he had asked about the grail, he would have cured the Fisher King, who had been wounded by a poisoned spear through the thigh (or the genitals). That's because the grail held a single wafer that could mysteriously sustain life indefinitely. (This might sound familiar too if you've read Susan Cooper's series *The Dark is Rising*, which has lots of Arthurian echoes.)

Because Perceval failed to cure the Fisher King, he had to go on a quest for the grail. Eventually he figured out that the Fisher King was his cousin. Lots of things happened to Perceval because he was so naïve about responsibility and chivalry, but he learned all sorts of life lessons along the way, and grew from simpleton to Grail Keeper because eventually he made it back with the grail, and cured the Fisher King. In other versions of the stories, Perceval had a lesser role, and a knight named Galahad became the grail hero.

The Holy Grail has been a topic of fascination for centuries. It represents a mystical experience that many people, including, T.S. Eliot, T.H. White and Alfred, Lord Tennyson have written about — the struggle between the forces of good and evil for possession of the grail, the most sacred of vessels. There are reams of interpretations of this story too. One is that the knights of a round table are Jesus' disciples, and when they search for the grail they're actually looking for a sacred relic, the cup Christ used at the Last Supper — the same cup that collected drops of divine blood during the crucifixion.

What's the longest word in the English language?

and Other Weird Answers About WORDS

93.

What's the longest word in the English language?

According to *The Oxford English Dictionary* it is the 45-letter word for a lung disease: pneumonoultramicroscopicsilicovolcanoconiosis.

The only other word with as many letters is: pneumonoultramicroscopicsilicovolcanoconioses. — which is just the plural form of the word!

In *Crazy English* Richard Lederer says the longest word has 1913 letters and stands for a chemical compound known in shorthand as Tryptophan Synthetase A Protein. (We'll pass on writing it out here.)

What other words are really long?
· At 28 letters, antidisestablishmentarianism, which means the doctrine against the dissolution of the establishment.
· At 29 letters, we have floccinaucinihilipilification, the categorizing of something as worthless or trivial.
· And at 30 letters, hippopotomonstrosesquipedalian, which — quite appropriately — means qualities pertaining to a long word.

94. What do you call words you can read both backwards and forwards?

Hannah L., Banff, Alberta

Words like *Bob*, *Mom*, *Hannah* and *madam*? They're called palindromes. Palindrome comes from a Greek word that means "running back again." The word was first used in English in 1629.

A palindrome is a word, phrase, number, sentence or series of sentences that read the same backward and forward. Palindromes can be small words or large, from: *mom, tot, peep, boob, madam, kayak, radar* and *reviver*, right up to *tattarrattat, kinnikinnik, detartrated* and *redivider*. Palindromic prime numbers include 101,131, and 313. Palindromes are not to be confused with something people do when they flip words backwards, like *stressed* for *desserts* or *drawer* for *reward*. Palindromes have to read the same both ways.

There is an old joke that Adam's first words to Eve were in the form of a palindrome, "Madam, I'm Adam." And it hasn't stopped since. Sotades supposedly discovered writing palindromically in the third century B.C. He wrote satiric verses . . . and met an untimely and bizarre end. Ptolemy II Philadelphus had Sotades sealed in a lead chest and dropped into the sea because Sotades had written a satire on him. Despite this cautionary tale, folks have been writing palindromically ever since.

Want to try your hand at this nutty obsession? You've got look at everything backward and try it out, as in *live* becomes *evil*. Then try working up to a small phrase: *Live not on evil; Dennis sinned; A Toyota; Stop pots.* Unfortunately, these sentences make little sense. The goal is a real (although often stupid) sentence, such as *Was it Eliot's toilet I saw?* Bonus points go for really rare ones — names such as *Mr. Alarm*, or complete stories, like: *Doc, note. I dissent. A fast never prevents a fatness. I diet on cod.*

One of the most famous palindromes is: *Able was I ere I saw Elba.* The story goes that Napoleon may have said this about the island, Elba, where he was exiled. But he didn't write it. Pity.

You won't get rich (or probably even hired) with this talent, but it can be fun. Most articles and prepositions are excluded in palindromes, since they don't work. The characteristic style of a palindrome is phrases that read like odd commands or sensational newspaper headlines. Here are some good ones:

A Santa at NASA
Stack Cats
Stella Won No Wallets
Sit on a Potato Pan, Otis
Must Sell at Tallest Sum
Ma Is a Nun, As I Am
Rats at a Bar Grab at a Star

Some read a bit more like an actual sentence, like the spectacular:

Go hang a salami! I'm a lasagna hog!

Or:

A man, a plan, a canal: Panama.

95. What's the meaning of "mind your p's and q's"?

Today it means that you need to behave yourself, and to act smartly for the situation. But that's a long way from where the saying started. Back in the seventeenth and eighteenth centuries the barmaids and bartenders in English alehouses were told to mind their p's and q's, which was short for pints and quarts (British units of measurement). In other words, be careful with how you pour that beer . . . or there will be no profits! Then, when it got rowdy, the bartender would tell customers to mind their own pints and quarts and settle down.

Typesetters who would set type by hand (long before the time of computerized typesetting) were also told to mind their p's and q's, since it was easy to mix up the two letters by reversing them. Check it out: *p* and *q* are mirror images.

96.

Why do people say things are "baloney"?

People may say things are baloney, and they might say they are boloney, but what they mean is that things are just not true — they are nonsense. Spelling it boloney is a better hint at a plausible answer. This word has probably been around since the 1870s, when there was a popular music hall song "I Ate the Boloney" (or the Bologna). Whatever the intention of the song was, eating Bologna means you eat a particular sort of smoked sausage made of a mix of leftover bits of all sorts of meats. Baloney (a slang version of Bologna) tends to be the staple for those who have to stretch their grocery dollars, and a favourite with children. It is inexpensive and tasty, but high in fat and made from lower quality meats. (Which leads us to that other saying: "No matter how thin you slice it — it's still baloney.")

So what does all of this mean? It means that calling something "baloney" means it is mixed up, or pretending to be more than it really is. In other words, nonsense.

Some other great words for baloney (as in "what a load of baloncy") are: hogwash, eyewash, hooey, malarkey, balderdash, foolishness, piffle, rot, humbug, jabberwocky, poppycock, bilge, folderol, gibberish, drivel, rubbish, bunk and babble.

Supercalifragilisticexpialidocious — what does it mean? Who made it up, and why?

Brian S., by e-mail

All 34 letters of this word were made up for the movie, *Mary Poppins*, by a writing team of two brothers, Bob and Dick Sherman. Their most famous song is "It's a Small World," which they wrote for the World's Fair in New York in 1964. You can hear it on the ride of the same name at Disneyland. The Shermans wrote all the songs for *Mary Poppins*, including "A Spoonful of Sugar," "Feed the Birds" and "Chim Chim Cher-ee." "Supercalifragilisticexpialidocious" means nothing, really. It is a very long nonsense word that is made up to sound like you are terribly smart and "you'll always sound precocious." Now we use it to mean that something is fantastic or super-fabulous.

Why do we say something is out of whack? What is "whack"?

David C., Seattle, Washington

"Whack" can mean many, many things. It is sometimes a verb, sometimes a noun. Here are some of its meanings (including the one you're asking about):

• a blow or the sound of a blow. It's a sharp powerful hit with the hand or fist. A famous use is the rhyme associated with a horrible 1892 crime:

Lizzie Borden took an ax
And gave her mother forty whacks;
And when she saw what she had done
She gave her father forty-one.

• a portion or a share as in: "He inherited a whack of cash."

• a state or condition. People in Great Britain might say, "I'm whacked," meaning exhausted.

• a chance to try something as in: "take a whack at it." A single occasion: "all at one whack."

• out of shape or out of order as in: "My back is out of whack," or "Since I drank that coffee I'm feeling out of whack."

• Slang for large or tremendous, as in: "Isn't the English language a whacking great marvel?"

99.

Where did "mind your own beeswax" come from?

Well, it does sound like "mind your own business," and it does mean that you should pay attention to your own issues, your own problems. But it came from a very surprising place — cosmetic history.

Some say the term comes from the days when smallpox was a common disease, and the resulting pockmarks (little irregular ugly holes) stayed on the face. Fine ladies would fill in the pockmarks with beeswax. The problem was that in warm weather, or if the lady got too close to the fire, the beeswax would melt. But it was considered rude to tell a lady that she needed to attend to her make-up — in the Victorian era wearing make-up wasn't considered proper, so the beeswax application was done in private and kept secret. If you mentioned it, you might get "mind your own beeswax" as a sharp response.

Index

Web sites of interest

Check out these Web sites for more information:

Platypus:
http://www.moonchildren.com/platypus/

Cricket:
http://www.srh.noaa.gov/elp/wxcalc/cricket.html

Leap day babies:
http://www.leapdaybabies.com
http://www.mystro.com/leap.htm

World records:
http://www.guinnessrecords.com

Hot water:
http://hepweb.rl.ac.uk/ppUK/PhysFAQ/hot_water.html

Video games:
http://www.videotopia.com/

Coriolis effect:
http://www.ems.psu.edu/~fraser/Bad/BadCoriolis.html

Ask Dr. Math:
http://forum.swarthmore.edu/dr.math/

Mars:
http://www.amnh.org/mars/

ACKNOWLEDGMENTS

Dr. Elizabeth Baerg, Vancouver, B.C.; Sandy Bogart Johnston, Markham, Ontario; Ewen Cameron, Massey University, New Zealand; Larry Campbell, Chief Coroner of British Columbia; Dick Canning, Naramata, B.C.; Dr. Hugh Chisholm, Atlantic Cat Hospital, Halifax, Nova Scotia; Dr. Janice Crook, North Vancouver, B.C.; Dr. Joel Ehrenkranz, Aspen, Colorado; Allistair Fraser, Professor of Meteorology, Penn State University; Margy Gilmour, Deep Cove, B.C.; Dr. Richard D. Granstein, Department of Dermatology, Cornell University, New York; Grace Hess, Vancouver, B.C.; Tina Holdcroft, Toronto, Ontario, for the illustrations; Brian Keating, The Calgary Zoo, Alberta; Natalie Linwong, Mt. Vernon, Illinois, for my favourite letter ever; Noel MacDonald, Vancouver, B.C.; Dr. Heather Meikle, Palmerston North, New Zealand; Joe Rubin, Toronto, Ontario; Carolyn Swayze, White Rock, B.C.; Catherine Ulibarri, Washington State University; Dr. Universe; the librarians at the Vancouver Public Library; Kathy Vey, Toronto, Ontario; John Vokes, Vancouver; Dr. Larry Wang, University of Alberta; Catherine Wedge, former Olympic equestrian, Vancouver, B.C.; Alexandra Woodsworth, Vancouver, B.C.

Photo by Lionel Trudel

Marg Meikle got the name The Answer Lady when she responded to people's wacky questions on CBC Radio's *The Gabereau Show*. She finds her answers wherever she can dig up the information — the Internet, the library, a CD-ROM database, or by getting in touch with an expert. She is the author of several books: *Dear Answer Lady, Return of the Answer Lady, Bumbering Around Vancouver* and *Garden City: Vancouver*. Check out Marg's latest kids' book with Scholastic: *Funny You Should Ask* answers 115 1/2 weird and wonderful questions.

Do YOU have a question?

You can e-mail the author at marg@meikle.com and check out www.dearanswerlady.com. You never know — *your* question, plus Marg's answer, could be included in a brand new book!